W9-BUE-546

Governance as Leadership

Governance as Leadership

Reframing the Work of Nonprofit Boards

RICHARD P. CHAIT
WILLIAM P. RYAN
BARBARA E. TAYLOR

BOARDSOURCE
Building Effective Nonprofit Boards

Formerly the National Center for Nonprofit Boards

WILEY
John Wiley & Sons, Inc.

Published by John Wiley & Sons, Inc., Hoboken, New Jersey.
Published simultaneously in Canada.

This publication is designed to provide accurate and authoritative informa-tion in regard to the subject matter covered. It is sold with the understand-ing that the publisher is not engaged in rendering professional services. If professional advice or other expert assistance is required, the services of a competent professional person should be sought.

Wiley also publishes its books in a variety of electronic formats. Some con-tent that appears in print may not be available in electronic books. For more information about Wiley products, visit our web site at www.wiley.com.

Library of Congress Cataloging-in-Publication Data:
ISBN 0-471-68420-1

Printed in the United States of America.

20 19 18 17 16 15

We collectively dedicate this book
to the memory of Judith O'Connor.

In addition,
we offer these personal expressions of gratitude:

In memory of Henry W. Sherrill,
my governance guru.
Richard Chait

To Sue, Nick, and Peter, for governance respite.
William Ryan

Always for David.
Barbara Taylor

Contents

About BoardSource

BoardSource is the premier resource for practical information, new ideas, and leadership development for board members of nonprofit organizations worldwide. Through highly acclaimed programs and services, BoardSource enables nonprofit organizations to fulfill their missions by helping build strong and effective boards. As the world's largest, most comprehensive publisher of materials on nonprofit governance, BoardSource offers a wide selection of books, videotapes, CDs, and online tools. BoardSource also hosts a biennial Leadership Forum, bringing together governance experts, board members, and chief executives of nonprofit organizations from around the world. In addition to workshops, training, and our extensive Web site, BoardSource governance consultants work directly with nonprofit leaders to design specialized solutions for organizations of all sizes working in diverse communities around the world. For more information, please visit www.boardsource.org, e-mail mail@boardsource.org, or call (202) 452-6262.

About the Authors

RICHARD P. CHAIT

Richard Chait, a professor at the Harvard Graduate School of Education, has studied nonprofit governance for more than 20 years. He has coauthored two books on the subject, *Improving the Performance of Governing Boards* (Oryx Press, 1996) and *The Effective Board of Trustees* (Oryx Press, 1993), as well as numerous articles including two in the *Harvard Business Review*, "The New Work of Nonprofit Boards" (September/October, 1996) and "Charting the Territory of Nonprofit Boards" (January/February, 1989). Chait also conducts research on faculty work life and academic leadership, most recently editing a volume on *The Questions of Tenure* (Harvard University Press, 2002).

Dr. Chait is a member of the Board of Directors of BoardSource and a trustee and member of the executive committee of the governing board of Wheaton College (MA). He was previously a trustee of Goucher College (MD) and Maryville College (TN). Chait has served as a consultant to the boards and executives of more than a hundred nonprofit organizations, particularly in education and the arts. In 2004, he was named one of Harvard University's "outstanding teachers."

WILLIAM P. RYAN

Bill Ryan is a consultant to foundations and nonprofit organizations and a research fellow at the Hauser Center for Nonprofit Organizations at Harvard University. His work focuses on nonprofit organizational capacity, primarily among human-service organizations. He has explored how several forces—including nonprofit access to capital, foundation grantmaking practices, competition with for-profit firms, and nonprofit governance—shape the capacity of nonprofits to deliver on their missions. Ryan is author or coauthor of a number of articles on these topics, including "The New Landscape for Nonprofits" and "Virtuous Capital: What Foundations Can Learn from Venture Capitalists" (both in *Harvard Business Review*), as well as *High Performance Nonprofit Organizations* (John Wiley & Sons, 1999). Before beginning his consulting practice in 1993, he worked in urban planning for nonprofit and government agencies in New York City.

BARBARA E. TAYLOR

Barbara Taylor is a senior consultant with the Academic Search Consultation Service, a nonprofit executive search firm whose clients include colleges, universities, and education-related nonprofits. Until 1996, Taylor was, for twelve years, director and then vice president for programs and research at the Association of Governing Boards of Universities and Colleges, an organization that serves trustees of higher education institutions.

Dr. Taylor is the author or coauthor of eight books, including *Improving the Performance of Governing Boards* (Oryx Press, 1996); *Strategic Indicators for Higher Education* (Peterson's, 1996); and *The*

Effective Board of Trustees (Oryx Press, 1993). She has also published numerous papers, book chapters, and case studies concerning governance, strategic planning, and institutional financial condition, including the *Harvard Business Review* articles, "Charting the Territory of Nonprofit Boards" and "The New Work of the Nonprofit Board." She has consulted with more than 100 nonprofit organizations on issues of governance, board-CEO and board-staff relations, and organizational assessment and planning. Taylor is a trustee emeritus of Wittenberg University.

Preface

Turn back the clock to 1986. One of the authors had an audience with a then education editor of the *New York Times* as part of a larger effort to kindle media interest in a study this researcher had just launched on college boards of trustees. Less than five minutes into the presentation, the editor interrupted to proclaim, "Governance is a yawner. What else are you working on?"

Today, governance has become a front-page story propelled by a steady flow of articles on acquiescent and negligent corporate boards, and unbridled (and often unethical) CEOs. A composite picture emerges that depicts boards of directors as insular, incestuous, and derelict. Nonprofit boards are under attack as well. Just within the last year, for instance, there have been notorious accounts about self-serving boards of family foundations, a university board that bungled a presidential search at great embarrassment and great cost ($1.8 million to settle with the president-elect), and a prominent independent school board that paid its headmaster a salary most outsiders regarded as indefensibly excessive.

In the wake of these various scandals, it is safe to say that almost everyone acknowledges the importance of governance, at least in theory. What is less clear is whether and how to make governing boards important in practice. BoardSource (formerly the National Center for Nonprofit Boards) has been at the forefront of these issues with a particular emphasis on feasible, valuable steps that trustees and CEOs can take to improve institutional governance. We were invited by BoardSource to consider whether nonprofit governance could benefit from fresh ideas as a complement to the organization's work on best practices. It is this topic, not governance mischief, which is the focal point of this book. In particular, we were motivated by four questions:

1. Why is there so much rhetoric that touts the significance and centrality of nonprofit boards, *but* so much empirical and anecdotal evidence that boards of trustees are only marginally relevant or intermittently consequential?

2. Why are there so many "how-to-govern" handbooks, pamphlets, seminars, and workshops, *but* such widespread disappointment with board performance and efforts to enhance board effectiveness?

3. Why do nonprofit organizations go to such great lengths to recruit the best and brightest as trustees, *but* then permit these stalwarts to languish collectively in an environment more intellectually inert than alive, with board members more disengaged than engrossed?

4. Why has there been such a continuous flow of new ideas that have changed prevailing views about organizations and leadership, *but* no substantial reconceptualization of nonprofit governance, only more guidance and exhortation to do better the work that boards are traditionally expected to do?

After many twists and turns, detours and dead ends, these four questions precipitated this book, one product of a larger

Governance Futures Project under the aegis of BoardSource and the Hauser Center for Nonprofit Organizations at Harvard University.

The book combines two familiar stories—one about leadership and the other about governance—into a new story about governance as leadership. Strangely enough, governance and leadership have not been linked before, almost as if each concept has a magnetic field that repels the other. (And remember that it is like poles, not opposites, that repel.) Nonprofits have organizational leaders and volunteer trustees. The former lead, the latter govern. We offer a different formulation: governance as leadership.

ONE RIVER, NOT TWO STREAMS

A vast intellectual enterprise—with thousands of trade and scholarly books and hundreds of professional development programs—has popularized the leadership story, generated new theory, and inspired new practices. The leadership story has many contributors: academic disciplines and professions as varied as psychology, sociology, political science, management, and education; reflections of successful practitioners; analyses of case studies; and comparative studies across cultures and nations. From these multiple sources, society has gained a far more sophisticated and complicated appreciation of leadership. At the very least, leadership is no longer viewed simplistically, based upon a single style, model, or aptitude (for example, intelligence, forcefulness, persuasiveness, or charisma). Instead, leadership has become a dynamic, multidimensional concept.

Similarly, the perfect organization was once defined as a smooth, efficient bureaucracy. Notions are more nuanced now. Both scholars and practitioners recognize, for instance, that organizations are also cultures (Deal and Kennedy, 1982), political systems (Baldridge, Curtis, Ecker, and Riley, 1978; Julius, Baldridge, and Pfeffer, 1999), dynamic organisms (Morgan, 1997), and open systems within a larger, competitive environment (Scott, 2003). Organizations also can be described metaphorically, for example, as theater (Bolman and Deal, 1997), organized anarchies (Cohen and March, 1974), learning organizations (Senge, 1990), loosely coupled systems (Weick, 1976), and cybernetic systems (Birnbaum, 1988a).

Now think about the language and metaphors of governance. They are notably impoverished, a sure sign that the fertile conversations about leadership and organizations have not yet incorporated governance or addressed the implications for boards. Currently, there is a narrow conception of boards as instruments of accountability and conservators (and sometimes suppliers) of tangible assets. The available images are mostly operational (for example, fiduciaries or authorizers) or unfavorable (for example, rubber stamps or micromanagers). There is no intellectual ferment that reconsiders trusteeship *in light of* new knowledge about leadership and organizations, as if, by analogy, breakthroughs in genetics had no relevance to the practice of medicine. In fact, trusteeship—conceptually and practically—seems to be remarkably unaffected by several generations of learning about leadership and organizations.

Most literature on trusteeship can be fairly categorized as either prescriptive or hortatory. There is little, if any, vibrant debate about what constitutes governance. The floor seems open primarily to relatively lifeless discussions about how to govern. Rather than challenge fundamental and popular notions—the very method that has advanced knowledge about leadership and organization—the tendency with governance has been to clarify and codify conventional practice. The conversation centers more around lists of "dos and don'ts" than around compelling or competing concepts of governance. While the concept of leadership has been illuminated, the concept of trusteeship has remained comparatively dim.

Given the very different epistemologies of leadership (and, by extension, organizations) on the one hand, and governance on the other hand, one might never guess that both stem from the same conceptual headwaters. Leadership theory runs swift and deep, the river banks crowded with animated commentators and interested observers. Governance theory trickles along the shallower backwaters; it attracts little notice and even fewer devotees. One stark statistic highlights the disparity: Barnes & Noble (Barnes & Noble, 2004) lists 27,220 books with the keyword "leader" or "leadership," compared to 2,349 with the keyword "trustee," "trusteeship," or "governance"—a 12:1 ratio.

Despite the differential output, leadership and governance are closely related, and the more clearly this linkage is seen, the brighter the prospects will be for better nonprofit governance. It is in this spirit that we treat governance and leadership not as separate stories that shape two distinct areas of practice, but as two intertwined plot lines in a much larger story about modern nonprofit organizations. We do not invent new theories about leadership or organizations; rather, we use these theories as catalysts to produce new concepts and practices about nonprofit governance. We turn next to who might find this larger story and these new notions of interest.

TARGET AUDIENCES

All three authors of this book are students of governance, consultants to boards, and trustees of nonprofit organizations. And at one time or another, we all worked as full-time administrators in not-for-profit institutions. Based on these experiences, we can explore governance from several angles and address the interests and concerns of people in all four of these roles.

While we aim to engage the interests of scholars and board consultants, the target audiences for this book are the nonprofit trustees, CEOs, and senior staff who meet Donald Schon's definition of reflective practitioners: people who "often think about what they are doing, sometimes even while doing it" (1983). These individuals, Schon continues:

> turn thought back on action and on the knowing which is implicit in action ... There is some puzzling, or troubling, or interesting phenomenon with which the individual is trying to deal. As he tries to makes sense of it, he also reflects on the understandings which have been implicit in his action, understandings which he surfaces, criticizes, restructures, and embraces in further action (1983).

In other words, this book will appeal most to nonprofit trustees and executives inclined not just to *do* governance, but to *understand* it as well—not to gain knowledge for its own sake but because they realize that a better understanding of governance leads to governing better. This, in turn, circles back to deeper understanding. As David Smith observed in *Entrusted: The Moral Responsibilities of Trusteeship*, effective boards "must become a reflective community of interpretation" where trustees "can and do talk seriously about organizational purpose" (1995) and, we would add, about the nature of governance. Conversely, trustees and staff who regard governing as little more than bright people using common sense and doing what comes naturally probably need read no further.

This book takes trustees and trusteeship seriously. We believe that board members want more than simple recipes for better trusteeship (for example, strengthen standing committees), deserve more than menus of maxims (for example, the board sets policy that management implements), and need more than a governance maven's advice *du jour* (for example, place the organization's mission statement on the back of business cards for trustees). Based on extensive personal experience with nonprofit boards throughout the sector, we are confident that trustees, with remarkably few exceptions, can understand and apply new thinking about governance. Governance does not need to be oversimplified; most board members—as professionals, executives, or community leaders—have already demonstrated the ability to grasp new ideas and handle complex situations.

Perhaps the greatest value will accrue to boards of trustees that read this book in tandem with their organization's CEO and then consider together what changes would improve the quality and centrality of institutional governance. Boards and CEOs are intertwined and interdependent. And while power struggles between the board and the chief executive officer may grab the headlines, more collaborative governance partners generally grab the brass ring. We do not advance here more precise delineations of the relative power and exclusive provinces of boards and executives. Countless efforts to do so have yielded either no fruit or bitter fruit because attempts to redistribute formal authority between the board and the CEO usually precipitate a zero-sum stalemate. However, initiatives to expand leadership opportunities for the board and the CEO, as we propose, promote better governance. At worst, challenges will not arise when a board or a CEO has too much authority, but rather when an organization has abundant sources of leadership to tap—a problem most nonprofits would welcome gladly.

We address this book to the not-for-profit sector at large, not at any one particular segment such as arts, education, environment, health care, or social services. While there certainly are differences among nonprofit organizations, for instance, history, mission, markets, strategy, and scale, the fundamental nature of governance and the essence of trusteeship are quite similar, if not universal, to the sector. Therefore, we write to a broad audience: nonprofits with volunteer boards and a professional staff.[1]

STRUCTURE OF THE BOOK

This book is divided conceptually into three parts. This and the next chapter provide a backdrop that sets the stage to view governance as tantamount to leadership. The next four chapters, which constitute the second part, describe the three modes of governance which, taken together, constitute governance as leadership. The first two of these four chapters cast familiar scenery in a new light as we discuss the fiduciary and strategic modes of governing. The next two place the generative mode, a less familiar concept of trusteeship, at center stage. In the final section of the book, we shift from ideas to action, and focus on practical, constructive steps that boards can take, with senior staff, to work effectively in the generative mode and to add greater value to the institutions they govern.

---

[1]The book does not address all-volunteer organizations and political associations. We also do not consider policies, laws, and regulations designed to demand better governance from nonprofit boards. While we appreciate the value (and limitations) of that approach, we focus on internally generated efforts boards can take toward the same objective: improved governance.

Chapter 1 outlines four "first principles" that emerged as important premises and pervasive themes of the book. We urge readers to start here as these ideas underlie all the chapters that follow.

Chapter 2 confronts and redefines the problems with non-profit boards. Whereas most literature on trusteeship addresses the problem of inadequate performance of boards, we treat this as symptomatic of a very different and more critical challenge: a problem of purpose.

Chapter 3 examines the most basic work of the board: the fiduciary mode. We consider the need to do fiduciary *work*, while avoiding the trap of becoming a fiduciary *board*, mired in the most traditional mode of governing. This chapter suggests that there is more to governing than stewardship of assets and more to fiduciary work than most boards appreciate.

Chapter 4 concerns the strategic mode, or the board's work vis-à-vis organizational strategy. We start with the more conventional view—boards as overseers of formal strategy—and then propose more consequential work where standard structures and processes are modified in order to focus the board on strategic thinking and action.

Chapter 5 introduces the concept of generative work—work that provides a new sense of the problems and opportunities at hand. We discuss the power of generative work and three processes by which to do it. The chapter makes the case that generative work, usually subsumed under the rubric of leadership, actually constitutes the essence of trusteeship—work best performed by the board in concert with the CEO.

Chapter 6 marks the transition from concept to practice, from generative work to generative governance. Here we present a set of integrated approaches to move up the generative curve where boards can do more work of greater import. Governing in the generative mode means looking for clues, operating at the organization's boundaries, framing issues, engaging the collective mind of the board in robust discussions, being forensic as well as futuristic, and tracking unconventional indicators of organizational performance.

Chapter 7 identifies the most valuable asset mix that trustees can contribute to governance as leadership. The chapter discusses four forms of capital—intellectual, reputational, political, and social—that trustees offer, and suggests how to generate and deploy this capital at a high rate of return to the organization.

In the final chapter, we offer executives and trustees some advice for starting their work with governance as leadership. Because most organizations are not starting with a blank slate, these final thoughts sketch the challenge of integrating governance as leadership into the organization's current structures and culture.

Acknowledgments

Quite simply, without the late Judith O'Connor, then CEO
and President of BoardSource, there would have been no
Governance Futures Project and no book entitled *Governance as
Leadership*. Judy recognized the need to infuse nonprofit governance with new concepts. She assembled the project team,
acquired the necessary resources, and offered invaluable advice
and constant encouragement.

We were the beneficiaries of wise counsel from others as
well, especially the Project Advisory Group, which included:
Christine Letts and Mark Moore of the Hauser Center for
Nonprofit Organizations at Harvard University, Judith Saidel
from the State University of New York at Albany, and Marla
Bobowick from BoardSource. We also profited from instructive
conversations with an array of noted theorists on leadership,
organizations, and nonprofit governance: Alan Altshuler, James
Austin, L. David Brown, Marion Fremont-Smith, Howard
Gardner, Steven Greyser, Daniel Halperin, James March, Henry
Mintzberg, Gareth Morgan, Charles Nesson, Jeffrey Pfeffer, Fred
Schauer, Frances Van Loo, and Christopher Winship. Early in the
project, we convened some very wise practitioners to "test
drive" a "concept car" we had designed. Based on the sage advice
we received from Susan Dentzer, Thomas Gottschalk, Raymond

Henze III, Thomas Jarom, Harold Jordan, David Nygren, Roger Raber, and Gary Walker, we returned to the drawing board with many improved ideas.

Early in our efforts to reassess the problems and potential of boards, we gained from the insights of the participants in the California Board Summit, cosponsored by BoardSource and the California Management Assistance Partnership. A group of experienced consultants to nonprofit boards assisted us in a similar pursuit: Mike Allison, Bob Andringa, Nancy Axelrod, Mike Burns, Denise Cavanaugh, Paul Connolly, Bruce Lesley, Chuck Loring, Fred Miller, Richard Novak, and Michela Perrone.

We are especially indebted to Jared Bleak, a recent doctoral student at the Harvard Graduate School of Education and now *Dr.* Bleak. Jared somehow managed to chronicle the two dozen or so disorderly discussions we had as a team over the life of the project. He also made important substantive contributions to our deliberations, tracked down scores of references and, not least, always made sure we, quite literally, had food for thought. Jared did all this with unfailing excellence, diligence, good will, and sharp wit.

As we approached the deadline for the manuscript, we were fortunate to enlist Megan Tompkins, an unusually able and meticulous graduate student at the Harvard Graduate School of Education, to fill in the blanks on many references and citations.

Finally, we are grateful for the generous support of The David and Lucile Packard Foundation, The Atlantic Philanthropies, the Surdna Foundation, and the W.K. Kellogg Foundation.

First Principles

We present here a set of first principles—basic premises that underlie the chapters that follow. Much like the overture to a Broadway show that can only be written after the composers have finished the score, we developed these principles toward the end, not the start, of the work that produced this book. These were not preconceived notions that generated predetermined content. To the contrary, this chapter appears first but was actually written last. We were only able to discern some first principles retrospectively because the propositions emerged as we discussed and drafted the other chapters. Only then did we notice some familiar refrains.

There are two ironies here. First, we maintain in Chapter 5 that organizations discover "emergent" strategies as well as design "deliberate" or planned strategies. Strategies, in effect, sneak up on organizations much as first principles sneak up on authors. Second, we contend in Chapter 5 that effective governance rests heavily on a board's capacity for retrospective "sensemaking"—acting and then thinking, making sense of past events to produce new meanings. We arrived at a new construct, *governance as leadership,* by writing and then reflecting, reframing, and revising—and by rethinking where governance stands today and why. While we never expressly intended to do so, the way we worked and the sense we made of governance echo the *leit-motif* of this book. The four principles summarized here distill recurrent themes and foreshadow arguments amplified in other chapters. To return to the analogy of the Broadway musical, these synopses are a medley, not the score.

PRINCIPLE ONE: NONPROFIT MANAGERS HAVE BECOME LEADERS

Nonprofit managers are not what they used to be, and most board members would probably respond "Thank goodness." Historically, the stereotypical image of a nonprofit administrator was a well-intentioned "do-gooder," perhaps trained as a social worker, educator, cleric, artist, or physician. The most successful practitioners—utterly unschooled about management, finances, investments, strategies, labor relations, and other "real world" realms—reluctantly, and sometimes accidentally, assumed greater managerial responsibility and eventually ascended to the top of the organization. Yesterday's naive nonprofit administrator or executive director has become today's sophisticated president or CEO, titles that betray changes in the stature, perception, and professionalism of the positions. (Likewise, staff have become "line officers" with such businesslike titles as vice president of marketing, strategy, technology, or knowledge management.)

Many executives have earned graduate degrees in nonprofit management from reputable universities; even more have attended executive education seminars and institutes on these same prestigious campuses. More important, nonprofit executives have acquired what formal education alone cannot confer: standing as organizational leaders (a status often underscored by the compensation package). As a result, trustees, employees, clients, and donors expect far more of nonprofit CEOs today than a genial personality, moral probity, managerial acumen, and a passionate commitment to the organization's social mission. Stakeholders, in a word, expect *leadership*.

Constituents expect nonprofit CEOs to articulate clearly and persuasively the organization's mission, beliefs, values, and culture. Both the process and the substance should galvanize widespread commitment toward these ends. With input from stakeholders inside and outside the organization, leaders are expected to shape agendas, not impose priorities; to allocate attention, not dictate results; and to define problems, not mandate solutions. These expectations we now have for leaders closely resemble conventional notions of *governing*.

In the not-for-profit context, governing means, to a substantial degree, engaging in these very activities. In theory, if not in practice, boards of trustees are supposed to be the ultimate guardians of institutional ethos and organizational values. Boards are charged with setting the organization's agenda and priorities, typically through review, approval, and oversight of a strategic plan. Boards are empowered to specify the most important problems and opportunities that management should pursue. If this logic holds, as we contend, then many nonprofit executives are not only leading their organizations, but by practicing this new version of leadership, they are actually governing them as well.

The transition from nonprofit administrators to organizational leaders has been almost universally heralded as a positive development. Almost everyone touts the value of leaders and, in any case, that is not at debate here. If, however, managers have become leaders, and leadership has enveloped core elements of governance, then a profound question arises: What have been the consequences to boards as the most powerful levers of governing have migrated to the portfolio and purview of leaders?

PRINCIPLE TWO: TRUSTEES ARE ACTING MORE LIKE MANAGERS

While nonprofit managers have gravitated toward the role of leadership, trustees have tilted more toward the role of management. The shift has occurred because (as described in the Preface) trusteeship, as a concept, has stalled while leadership, as a concept, has accelerated. The net effect has been that trustees function, more and more, like managers.

This will no doubt strike many as an unlikely claim since the number one injunction of governance has been that boards should not meddle or micromanage. Despite this oft-repeated admonition, much of the prescriptive literature on trusteeship actually focuses squarely on operational details: budgets, audits, facilities, maintenance, fundraisers, program reviews, and the like. To discharge that work, most boards structure committees around the portfolios of line officers: finance, development, government relations, program evaluation, and customer/client relations, for example. Moreover, management competence typically ranks high on the list of desired attributes of prospective trustees. Nonprofits usually want a Noah's ark of professional experts. As a result, many boards resemble a diversified consulting firm with specialties in law, labor, finance, marketing, strategy, and human resources. Constructed and organized in this way, boards are predisposed, if not predestined, to attend to the routine, technical work that managers-turned-leaders have attempted to shed or limit.

With sophisticated leaders at the helm of nonprofits, a substantial portion of the governance portfolio has moved to the executive suite. The residue remains in the boardroom. This surprise twist in the story line suggests that the real threat to nonprofit governance may not be a board that micro*manages,* but a board that micro*governs,* attentive to a technical, managerial version of trusteeship while blind to governance as leadership.

This quandary of *migratory governance* could be viewed as a winner-take-all joust between the CEO as the leader and the board as a source of leadership. Or the problem could be framed as a zero-sum contest in which trustees must forego the "bread and butter," canonical components of governance (for example, finances, facilities, strategy, and development) in order to reclaim from executives a significant measure of influence over the most potent facets of governance (for example, mission, values, beliefs, culture, agendas). However, the formulation of governance as leadership provides a more affirmative and constructive approach that expands the pie, provides more occasions and levers for leadership, and enhances the trustees' value to the organization. Just as significantly, governance as leadership enhances the organization's value to trustees. Board members will become more fulfilled and less frustrated as opportunities multiply for meaningful engagement in consequential issues. Toward that end, governance must be recast from a fixed and unidimensional practice to a contingent, multidimensional practice with three distinct yet complimentary modes. In other words, governing is too complicated to reduce to simple aphorisms, however seductive, like "boards set policies which administrators implement" or "boards establish ends and management determines means."

Although new when applied to governance, "complexity" is now routinely accepted in other realms. In fact, "complexity science" (Zimmerman, Lindberg, and Plsek, 1998) and "complex systems" (Scott, 2003) have already entered the lexicon of organizational behavior. There are two obvious analogues to governance. First, "intelligence" once denoted analytical horse-power. Then, Howard Gardner introduced the concept of "multiple intelligences" (1983) which conceptualized personal competence as a varied repertoire. Intelligence could be denom-inated as linguistic, logical, spatial, kinesthetic, musical, inter-personal, and intrapersonal.[1] Second, leadership over the years has been (almost sequentially) associated with certain physical attributes and personality traits, then with power and influence, then with specific realms of expertise (for example, interper-sonal skills, analytical skills, financial acumen), and then with particular activities (for example, planning, decision making). Now both theoreticians and practitioners realize that effective leaders are "cognitively complex" (Birnbaum, 1992), that is, able to think and work effectively and concurrently in multi-ple modes: for instance, as managers, entrepreneurs, politicians, visionaries, analysts, learners, icons, and culture makers.

Effective leaders move seamlessly from mode to mode as conditions warrant. Executives do not simply learn one mode or even two and then employ that mode regardless of the situ-ation. Regrettably, trustees often do just that.

PRINCIPLE THREE: THERE ARE THREE MODES OF GOVERNANCE, ALL CREATED EQUAL

We posit that there are three modes of governance that com-prise governance as leadership:

- Type I—the *fiduciary mode,* where boards are concerned primarily with the stewardship of tangible assets

---

[1]Gardner (1993) later proposed naturalist, spiritual, and existential intelli-gence and Goleman (1995) popularized "emotional intelligence."

- Type II—the *strategic mode,* where boards create a strategic partnership with management
- Type III—the *generative mode,* where boards provide a less recognized but critical source of leadership for the organization.

When trustees work well in all three of these modes, the board achieves governance as leadership.

Each type emphasizes different aspects of governance and rests on different assumptions about the nature of organizations and leadership. However, *all three types are equally important;* each fulfills vital purposes. Types I and II are, at present, the dominant modes of nonprofit governance; Type III is the least practiced (see Exhibit 1.1).

Type I constitutes the bedrock of governance—the fiduciary work intended to ensure that nonprofit organizations are faithful to mission, accountable for performance, and compliant with

EXHIBIT 1.1   GOVERNANCE AS LEADERSHIP: THE GOVERNANCE TRIANGLE

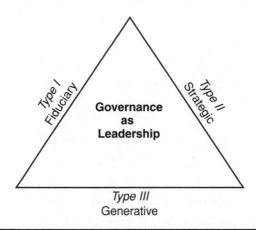

Type I
Fiduciary

Type II
Strategic

Governance as Leadership

Type III
Generative

relevant laws and regulations. Without Type I, governance would have no purpose. If a board fails as fiduciaries, the organization could be irreparably tarnished or even destroyed. Type II concerns the strategic work that enables boards (and management) to set the organization's priorities and course, and to deploy resources accordingly. Without Type II, governance would have little power or influence. If a board neglects strategy, the organization could become ineffective or irrelevant.

Types I and II are undeniably important forms of governance. However, boards that *only* oversee assets and monitor strategy do work that is necessary but not sufficient to maximize the value of governance (generally) and the value of trustees (more particularly).

As one moves through the chapters that follow, it may appear that we assign greater importance to the generative mode or, at a minimum, that we position Type III as the first among equal modes. In truth, we assert no hierarchy of modes, and we do not advocate that boards abandon or neglect Types I and II. To the extent that we elevate Type III to prominence (and we do devote more attention to Type III), we do so not because Type III trumps I and II, but because the generative mode is less recognizable to nonprofit trustees and executives than the other modes and thus requires more elaboration. The disproportionate attention owes to the relative novelty, not the relative worth, of Type III vis-à-vis Types I and II.

PRINCIPLE FOUR: THREE MODES ARE BETTER THAN TWO OR ONE

A board's effectiveness increases as the trustees become more proficient in more modes. If the term "triple threat"—high praise for an athlete—did not carry a negative connotation when attached to governing boards, we would adopt this phrase to convey the idea that exemplary boards perform skillfully in all three modes. Instead, we make do with "tri-modal."

In any case, a board that excels in one mode (or two) but flounders in another one (or two) will add far less value to an organization than a board that ably executes all three. Trustees quick to exhort the staff to outwit, outwork, and even outspend the competition might consider an additional tactic: *outgovern* the competition. The greatest comparative advantage will accrue to "tri-modal" boards. In order to create more value, boards of trustees need to "cross-train" so that the "muscle memory" of one mode does not dominate to the detriment of the others. (This is one reason why world-class weightlifters are usually inept basketball players.) When boards overemphasize one mode to the exclusion of others (a common problem), the net results are worse, not better, governance.

The majority of boards work most of the time in either the fiduciary or strategic mode. These are comfortable zones for trustees. Nonetheless, many boards neither overcome the inherent challenges that Types I or II pose nor capitalize on the occasional leadership opportunities that fiduciary and strategic governance present. As a result, some of the board's potential to add value goes untapped, despite the trustees' familiarity with the mode. However, there may be an even steeper price to pay if boards overlook or underperform Type III work because, unlike Types I and II where there are moments for leadership, the generative mode is about leadership. It is the most fertile soil for boards to flower as a source of leadership.

Chapters 3 and 4 on Types I and II challenge boards to do better at what boards normally do; no one should discount the value of continuous, incremental improvements as applied to trusteeship. By contrast, Chapters 5 and 6 on Type III invite (some might say compel) boards to invent new governance practices. Taken together, all three modes encourage nonprofit trustees and executives to combine ideas and practices, some familiar, others novel, into a new approach: *Governance as Leadership.*

CHAPTER 2

Problem Boards or Board Problems?[1]

There is no question that the nonprofit sector has a board problem. Frustration with boards is so chronic and widespread that *board* and *troubled board* have become almost interchangeable. When we describe boards it is often to distinguish one bad one from another: Letterhead board or micromanaging board? Founder's board or rubber-stamp board? And when a nonprofit executive says, "I have a really good board," savvy listeners know this often means "I have a compliant board." The confessions of board members are equally disheartening. Many find serving on boards to be an exercise in irrelevance, summed up in two questions many trustees ask themselves: "Why am I here?" and "What difference do I make?" Of course, there is more at stake than boredom. The board appears to be an unreliable instrument for ensuring accountability—the outcome society most wants from it. Behind every scandal or organizational collapse is a board (often one with distinguished members) asleep at the switch. And while it is true that a board is behind every high-

---

[1]Parts of this chapter were published in *The Nonprofit Quarterly,* Summer 2003.

performing organization, it is often along for the ride, cheering and boosting the work of the executive and staff.

A cottage industry (in which the authors toil) has emerged to help nonprofits deal with these problems. Training programs, consulting practices, academic research, and practical guidebooks all promise a way out of the morass. Virtually all of these solutions are based on the same diagnosis of board problems. And because a solution can be no better than the diagnosis that precedes it, we start in this chapter with the diagnostic consensus of the board-improvement field. We conclude that the field has been working on the wrong problem, or, more precisely, that we have mistaken a part of the problem for the whole. In order to develop better solutions, we need a better picture of the problem.

PROBLEMS OF PERFORMANCE

Most diagnoses in the board-improvement field focus on three prevalent problems of *performance*. First, both board members and analysts have long believed that the common dysfunctions of groups—rivalries, domination of the many by the few, one-way communication, and bad chemistry—prevent effective deliberating and decision making by boards. The father of the nonprofit board-improvement industry, General Henry M. Robert, found disorderly discourse to be the biggest problem facing the boards and associations he served in the nineteenth century. Some dominated the discussion, conversations were endless, or both. With intimidating detail, he tried to remedy these group-dynamic problems with the now famous *Robert's Rules of Order* (Robert III, Evans, Honemann, and Balch, 2000). Our conception of successful group work has changed over the years. Rather than parliamentary procedure, we are more apt to encourage free-flowing discussions and to try team-building exercises that promote trust, commitment, and collaboration. But the group-dynamic diagnosis remains.

Second, board members are frequently faulted for being disengaged. They are faulted for not knowing what is going on in their organizations and for not demonstrating much desire to find out. Attendance at board meetings is often spotty and participation perfunctory. The disengagement problem has inspired its own hackneyed images: "no-show trustees" and board members who "check their brains at the door." Analysts have suggested a variety of carrots and sticks to improve the situation. The idea of paying nonprofit trustees, though rarely practiced, is periodically proposed. Some organizations try to increase psychic and social rewards, with more opportunities for gratifying contact with clients, more interesting social interactions with fellow trustees and donors, and (occasionally) more direct benefits like favored treatment for family and friends. In recruiting, some boards actually encourage the disengagement they later lament: They promise prospective board members that there will be little work to do, in the hope that low expectations will attract more prospective board members. Policy makers and legal analysts have argued that the solution lies outside the board room. Some argue that if laws were changed to make board members personally liable for a wider variety of organizational failures, then trustees would pay more attention. Others argue the opposite—that liability *discourages* service on nonprofit boards, and that trustees should be shielded from such risks ("Volunteer Protection Act of 1997," 1997).

But a third problem—more than any other—has captured the imagination of the board-improvement field and inspired many common solutions. In this diagnosis, boards do not perform well because they do not know what their job is. When we discussed with 28 nonprofit governance consultants their recent engagements with troubled boards, 19 characterized the client's problem as ignorance of or confusion about roles and responsibilities. Dozens of analysts have offered one version or another of an "official job description" for the board. This prescriptive literature can be distilled into five functions:

1. Set the organization's mission and overall strategy, and modify both as needed.
2. Monitor organizational performance and hold management accountable.
3. Select, evaluate, support, and—if necessary—replace the executive director or CEO.
4. Develop and conserve the organization's resources—both funds and facilities.
5. Serve as a bridge and buffer between the organization and its environment; advocate for the organization and build support within the wider community.

This roles-and-responsibilities approach to board performance has obvious appeal. With the problem defined as confusion about roles and responsibilities, the solution becomes clarity, and the holy grail becomes an unambiguous official job description. Ironically, in most work environments, the specificity of job descriptions increases as one *descends* the organization chart. Yet, here, nominally at the top of the organizational pyramid, trustees and executives seem to think that nonprofit organizations need only specify the board's role to cure the board's problem. In effect, boards can codify their way out of board problems.

The official job description is a reasonable point of departure to address the problems of new boards or inexperienced trustees. Even more established boards, with members who should know better, can drift into seductive but random activities that create little or no value for their organizations. Revisiting the official job description probably helps them, too. But the frustration with nonprofit boards, and *of* nonprofit board members, is not about inexperience. The bigger problem is the disappointing performance of mature boards with seasoned members. These are talented individuals and experienced trustees; their feeble performance is therefore especially disheartening. The conventional problems of performance—particularly confusion about roles and responsibility—offer an inadequate diagnosis.

FROM PROBLEMS OF PERFORMANCE
TO PROBLEMS OF PURPOSE

We contend that another problem looms behind these problems of performance: a more fundamental problem of *purpose*. Some advocates of the roles-and-responsibilities approach inadvertently acknowledge the problem of purpose when they reason that the board must be important since it endures as an institution. "The widespread existence of boards," wrote Cyril Houle, "means they must possess values which are apparently essential to modern life. It will therefore be useful to assess the reasons why boards are important" (1960). The very formulation of this approach raises a troubling question. If the board is so important, why is a whole literature required to explain *why* it is so important? What if one of the central problems plaguing the board is not, in fact, uncertainty about its important roles and responsibilities, but rather a lack of compelling purpose in the first place? We maintain that many board members are ineffectual not just because they are *confused* about their role but because they are *dissatisfied* with their role. They do not do their job well because their job does not strike them as worth doing well. In other words, we believe that board members themselves—in asking "Why am I here?" and "What difference do I make?"—have offered the best diagnosis of all.

This diagnosis is more illuminating if one asks not just *whether* boards are vulnerable to problems of purpose but *where*. Is the problem with the board's most important, official governing work? Or with less important, unofficial work? If governance is the use of authority to set an organization's purposes and to ensure it serves those purposes effectively and efficiently, then it follows that some of what boards do is not actually governing. Informal coaching of a CEO, advising and troubleshooting with staff outside of board meetings, volunteering on the front lines of service delivery—boards might perform these functions, and they might inform a board's governing, but they are not governing per se. They represent unofficial, though not unimportant, work.

Even among the board's official governing assignments, it is possible to deem some duties more essential than others. To make this distinction, it helps to ask which duties one can imagine a board delegating entirely—either to staff or consultants—and still claim to be governing the organization. Farming out fundraising and community relations (both of which are often shared among staff, consultants, and celebrity ambassadors) does not threaten governance in a fundamental way. But a board that outsources mission setting or management oversight is highly problematic, as troubling as a government that puts legislating or judicial sentencing out to bid along with trash hauling and street cleaning. Yes, it is all government or, in this case, governance. But some is more essential than the rest.

With these distinctions in mind, we can offer a refined diagnosis: Boards are vulnerable to problems of purpose both in their official and their unofficial work. As result, it is not just trustee satisfaction that is at risk but also effective governing. Consider four manifestations of the purpose problem:

Some Official Work Is Highly Episodic

Most people take little account of the fact that much of the official work of the board is highly episodic. There is not, thankfully, always a CEO to hire or fire, or a major question of mission to consider. Yet board members meet at regularly prescribed intervals as if there *were* always important governing work to do. In most fields where important work is episodic, practitioners do not insist (or pretend) otherwise. Effective fire companies are not always fighting fires; fire departments put their downtime to good use—engaging in training, maintenance, and fire prevention. The same cannot be said for boards.

By denying the episodic reality of governing work, boards back into a problem of purpose. If there are no urgent matters of governance before the board, meetings are devoted to presenting routine committee reports. To ward off this boredom, many organizations have begun over-relying on the board's role as strategy maker—cramming the agenda with as many interesting strategy questions as possible. Many boards now *expect* agendas replete with "bet-the-company" questions. To meet this demand for strategic content, staff sometimes inflate routine issues into questions of strategy. Before long, board members and staff alike begin to equate *meeting* with *governing*. It is at these meetings where everything comes wrapped in strategy, but where little or nothing truly important is at stake, that board members start to wonder, "What difference am I making?"

Ironically, the most valued contributions of board members often come during downtime—when there is no indispensable governing work to do. For example, we frequently ask board members to think about a "no-board scenario" by posing the following question: "What would be the single gravest consequence to your organization if your board did not meet or conduct board business in any way for a two-year period?"The most common responses are the loss of fundraising capacity, loss of good advice or expertise, and loss of contacts in the community. Over the course of these two hypothetical years without a board, few people fear the result will be mission drift, strategic blunder, or a compromising of core values.They acknowledge, in effect, that the board's essential governing work is episodic, but that it does other important work in the interim. Unfortunately, the structure and culture of most boards precludes this acknowledgement:Trustees keep right on meeting, even as they are disappointed by the lack of meaning in their work

Some Official Work Is Intrinsically Unsatisfying

Not all of the board's governing work is episodic. Overseeing and monitoring the organization's managers—to spot problems or malfeasance—is ongoing and critically important.The "monitoring and oversight" duty in the official job description is really a response to the fundamental legal demand that society makes of boards. By law, boards are to be responsible to the

broader community for what their organizations do—and especially for what they do wrong. The law demands that boards
meet their "duties of loyalty and care," which means focusing on
norms and standards of *minimally acceptable* behavior. In effect,
trustees are tasked to prevent trouble rather than promote success. But their method for doing this compounds the problem
of purpose: Routine oversight is hardly engaging.

In fact, a job designed primarily for oversight violates virtually all we know about motivation. Board members, in particular, join organizations because of the meaning the affiliation
provides. They identify with and want to support the mission,
cause, or values of the organization (Taylor, Chait, and Holland,
1991). Who has ever been moved to join a board thinking, "I
really want to hold this organization to account?" But this is, of
course, a good part of what the job demands. And while people
might agree to *join* in order to affiliate with a mission, they are
more apt to *participate* when they can see the results of their
work and the opportunity to have influence. Here again, oversight activity is a disappointment. Oversight is more looking
than finding. And the work of looking is often technical—
scrutinizing budgets, financial statements, or construction plans—
and often tedious to boot. It is as if eager Peace Corps volunteers
arrived at their posts only to find their main job was to ensure
that foreign aid was not misspent.

In effect, by constructing their job around the fiduciary work
of oversight, nonprofit organizations have placed board members in a position akin to that of a substitute teacher. As an *institution,* the substitute teacher works effectively. It assures school
administrators and parents that children who might run amok
in the absence of a teacher remain under control. But the *work*
of the substitute teacher is singularly unattractive. Adherence to

minimum standards—not trying to teach, but merely trying to keep order—is as (or more) challenging than actually teaching. It is also far less rewarding. Board members suffer from this *substitute's dilemma*. Society has essentially asked trustees to keep order. As a result, board members become disengaged. The more disengaged they become, the less likely trustees are to ensure accountability—the very reason we created boards in the first place. By asking for a little, we get even less.

If the problem of purpose is most acute with the board's official governing work, it is tempting to conclude that looking for *un*official work might provide sufficient appeal to keep board members engaged in their essential governing work. And to some extent, this is what boards commonly do. But this path to meaningful engagement is blocked on two fronts.

Some Important Unofficial Work Is Undemanding

Some of the board's most important unofficial work does not really depend on the efforts of individual board members, and therefore does not provide them with opportunities for meaningful engagement. This partly explains why boards can be so important to their organizations yet so unrewarding for their own members. This type of work poses for board members the predicament of the monarch in a modern, democratically governed state. While the *institution* of the monarchy helps create a national identity, reassures and unifies the country in times of crisis, marks important events through ceremony, and develops the tourism economy, the *individual* monarch deserves little credit for any of these results. And to the extent that the work involves endless ribbon cuttings, award ceremonies, and grand parades, there is not much stimulation either. Boards and board members are similar in at least three respects:

First, a board can create *legitimacy* for an organization. Unlike the business sector, where stakeholders can judge a corporation by financial performance, observers in the nonprofit sector tend to rely on a number of proxies to determine what constitutes a good organization. Potential funders, clients, and even employees look at an organization's board—especially if it is a distinguished one—as evidence of legitimacy. They are far more apt to ask "Who is on your board?" than "What does your board do?" Board members need not *do* anything to create legitimacy—beyond lending their names to the organization's letterhead and occasionally attending a public function or official event associated with the organization. The board's very existence creates legitimacy.

Similarly, the board provides managers what organizational theorists call "sense-making opportunities" *simply by meeting* (see Chapter 5). The mere prospect of a board meeting—where little or nothing may actually happen—forces managers to prepare written and oral reports that make sense of organizational events, recent challenges, and data about performance. Management must be able to communicate to the board an integrated and sensible account that describes and interprets the organization's situation. Presumably, a more inquisitive board will compel managers to be better sense-makers, but the mere occasion of board meetings goes a long way by itself. A board meeting could be canceled at the last minute and something good—more thoughtful and focused management—would still have resulted.

As an entity, the board also encourages *vigilance by managers.* Nonprofit executives often say, "The board keeps me on my toes" or "I can feel the board looking over my shoulder." As useful as this is to the organization, keeping managers "on their toes" is not likely to be engaging for board members, any more than state troopers find it stimulating to park at the side of the road because their mere presence slows traffic. Troopers can keep drivers on their toes while they themselves are literally asleep at the wheel.

Some Unofficial Work Is Rewarding but Discouraged

If official work is too episodic or tedious, and if some unofficial work is more institutional than personal, board members have the option of participating in other, more gratifying unofficial work. Boards of new organizations, even organizations with full-time staff, participate routinely in much of the hands-on, day-to-day work of the organization. As a result, they know why they are there and what difference they make. In doing this work, however, board members are repeatedly reminded that they must not cross the line into "micromanaging" or "meddling."

The rules about what constitutes permissible board work are somewhat mysterious. Fundraising, advocacy, and community relations make the short list of official duties, but human-resource management and program development do not. Why? It is true that organizations can never have too much money or influence, or too many friends. Board members are often good at fundraising and community relations; they generally perform these roles ably and willingly. But these are not, as we suggested earlier, absolutely essential governing duties. Board members are not uniquely qualified for this work; managers often perform both functions alongside board members. Why, then, are trustees not guilty of meddling in these instances? Probably because they keep board members busy *outside* the organization, where they are far less prone to interfere with the work of managers and staff. More than a coherent theory about the division of policy and administration, the rules of board engagement seem to be rooted in an understandable desire on the part of management to assure a measure of professional discretion and even autonomy, and to have trustees marshal resources for the organization to do what management intends.

■ ■ ■

Our diagnosis of the problem as purpose makes the situation look much worse than the more prevalent diagnosis of performance. In our analysis, boards may know what to do, and do it reasonably well, but in the end they are derailed by the meaninglessness of what they do. Worse, it is not that some incidental parts of the job happen to be tiresome now and then: The problems of purpose are most acute when the board's key governing work is involved. And the option of promoting engagement by giving boards more unofficial work only raises other problems of purpose.

THE CHALLENGE OF REFORM

If the problem is purpose, then the diagnosis begs for a new and improved official job description—one that assigns boards a more attractive array of tasks and might even inspire new ways of organizing those tasks into new board structures. This is precisely what we need to resist.

A task-and-structure approach is fraught with risks. First, a more appealing set of tasks might lead to busier, even happier boards, but not necessarily to better governed organizations.

Not everything a board does or can do is governing. And our goal should not be busier boards but rather more effective governing. Second, focusing on board tasks tends to encourage the microgoverning that has marginalized many boards in the first place. Tasks are prescribed and performed. So the more easily board tasks can be specified and the more routinely they can be performed, the more likely they are to represent a technical, managerial version of governance. Third, as virtually any workplace experience confirms, task clarification does not always promote effectiveness. Can any of us name the job where we succeeded primarily by focusing diligently on our job description? In fact, is there a better indicator of imminent failure than the sight of someone studying his job description for guidance?

Creating structures to coordinate board tasks has similar limitations. An organizational chart or, in this case, a board's committee structure, does answer important questions about who has authority over what issues and who has responsibility for what tasks. But organizational charts hardly ensure effective work. One might study them to see how organizations hope to work, but not to see how they *actually* work, much less how *well* they work.

Nevertheless, the task-and-structure approach remains appealing for understandable reasons. If the answer to board problems is *not* in enumerating clearly delineated tasks and building fixed committee structures around them, then the search for better boards might force us into very murky territory: relying on board members' personal judgment, artistry, or wisdom. If assembling naturally gifted or richly experienced board members is the only way to improve boards, then our prospects for large-scale change—with 1.5 million nonprofit organizations currently in place and more forming every year—soon look bleak.

But because the task-and-structure approach also offers a circular logic, it is hard to envision alternatives to it. Together, task and structure seem like the sum total of governance. They supply good answers to our most important governing questions: What *is* governing? And how does a board do it? In response, boards tend to envision governance as the sum of discrete goal-setting or oversight tasks—hiring and firing, planning, reviewing, evaluating, and so on—structured as a series of committees. These tasks and structures explain how to govern, by which we mean how to use authority to (a) set an organization's goals and purposes and (b) ensure the organization's resources are deployed efficiently and appropriately. There seems little need to look beyond task and structure and no clue about where to start if a board wanted to.

An alternative logic begins to emerge if we ask a different question. In addition to asking "What is governing?" we can ask "What is it we're governing?" In other words, do the types of governing that boards practice work for the types of organizations they have? The idea of an organization–governance gap surfaced when we sought advice on governance problems from trustees, executives, consultants, and researchers. Some of them suggested that current board structures might be a bad fit for today's nonprofit organizations. To overstate only a little, the idea that we govern today's nonprofits with the same model introduced nearly 400 hundred years ago to govern Harvard College, their colonial forerunner, troubled these observers. They cited the emergence of entrepreneurial organizations, interorganizational alliances, and multicorporate forms (for example, nonprofits with subsidiaries), and argued that these new organizational structures might require new board structures for governing.

The nonprofit governance literature has long recognized another gap—a gap between the demands of an organization at a particular point in its life cycle on the one hand and the composition of and governing approaches of its board on the other. The board of a young organization, according to this analysis, faces challenges that boards of older organizations do not, like establishing the legitimacy of the organization and launching fundraising efforts to help it survive the first fragile years of a start-up. These developmental and structural gaps pose an important question. What do organizations demand of governing?

In this spirit, we want to explore another potential gap—one between our *mental maps* of organizations and the *governing modes* we use. While no one refers to a formal theory of the modern organization to get through the day, we do consult our own personal theories of organization in order to navigate the work world. These are the assumptions, beliefs, convictions, and hypotheses that help us make sense of what happens in the organizations where we work. These personal theories are like the "mental maps" that sociologists study to understand people based on the way they depict their neighborhoods. A good street map will tell us what we need to know about a neighborhood's layout, but the mental maps of local residents tell us what people value in that neighborhood and how they inhabit it. When residents draw their own maps, we can learn from the boundaries they choose and the landmarks by which they navigate. Some organize their environment around churches, others around restaurants. Some place the border of their own neighborhood and adjacent ones based on demographics, others set boundaries based on subway lines.

Official job descriptions and organizational charts define and distribute tasks across the organization. In contrast, our mental maps of organizations help us choose management or leadership *modes,* or cognitive approaches, suitable to workplace challenges. By describing what—*in addition to the structures and hierarchies of organizations*—really makes organizations tick, our mental maps suggest appropriate work modes. Some see organizations as political systems, where continuous negotiations are essential. Some see them as social networks, where who you know is more important than what you know. Some see them as machines, where reliable production of quality outputs is the goal. (Some see them as Dilbert-like zones of mindlessness, where coping is the only goal.) Most often, of course, people are eclectic and see their organizations as a blend of these. To respond to these different dimensions of organizational life, we need modes of managing and leading, not tasks and structures.

Leaders are expected to choose a mode that fits their organization or organizational situation. Consider a hypothetical CEO who concludes that his organization has become too decentralized. He is likely to respond to the challenge of centralizing operations by working in multiple modes, rather than by merely performing a series of tasks. In addition to reconfiguring procedures say, to approve budgets, programs, and personnel appointments, he may conclude there is political work to do to reassure colleagues who are wary of a power grab. There might be symbolic work to do to create a greater sense of common enterprise. There might be tactical work to do to develop a new incentive structure for cooperation. The modes he works in depend on how he sees organizations in general and the organizational situation at hand in particular.

Not surprisingly, mental maps have inspired learning, experimentation, and innovation in both the theory and practice of leadership. Leaders have had new insights into the nature of organizations—new mental maps—and come up with new leadership approaches in response. Theorists have come up with their own insights about the nature of organizations, often by documenting the work of these leaders. In both cases, instead of asking "What is leadership?" and "How do we lead?" they ask: "What are organizations, and what do they demand of leaders?"

Governance, meanwhile, has been slumbering peacefully. People who study organizations rarely give much thought to governance, and people who study governance seldom think much about organizations. We learned this when we made pilgrimages to some eminent organizational theorists. They had generously agreed to discuss how their insights into organizations—now enshrined in MBA curricula, consulting practices worldwide, and the personal habits of legions of managers and leaders—illuminate the problems of boards.

Our conversations were short, and followed the same pattern. An innovative theorist on power in organizations explained that he rarely felt the urge to look at boards since they have so little influence on organizations. Henry Mintzberg, a leading theorist on strategy, likened boards to bumblebees buzzing around the heads of CEOs. A theorist on organizational behavior, when asked how he pictured boards, answered: "As window dressing. But I mean that in the best possible way." And to review the literature on governance is to see the mirror image of this phenomenon: Few of the prescriptions for nonprofit boards have much to say about the nature of the organizations that boards are presumed to govern.

What if they did? The implications for governance would be enormous. For one, they would see that, in addition to the fixed goals and tasks of fiduciary and strategic work, Types I and II governing (as defined in Chapter 1 and detailed in Chapters 3 and 4) call for governing in fiduciary and strategic *modes*—choosing and using different cognitive approaches. More important, it would be clear that these two are not complete, that organizations, as conceptualized today, call for a third mode of governing.

Everyone is familiar with the goals of Type I—to ensure an organization's resources are used efficiently and effectively in pursuit of its mission. Everyone is also familiar with the tasks of Type I—audits and oversight routines. Less familiar is the idea of Type I as a mode, or a cognitive approach, that boards choose to use sometimes to govern some aspects of an organization but not others. This is in part because the mental map of Type I is rarely examined. If one were to ask what kind of organization demands fiduciary governing, it would be the *productive, machine-like* organization that converts resources into assets and deploys those assets to advance the organization's goals as efficiently and effectively as possible. And although all organizations aspire to be productive and also have machine-like aspects, there is more to them than that.

The strategic mode addresses another aspect of governing and focuses on other aspects of organizations. Again, the goals and tasks of Type II are familiar. The goal is to figure out how to get an organization from its present to its preferred future. The tasks are the steps of formal strategic planning—whether it be SWOT analysis (Kotler and Murphy, 1991) or the construction of a series of logical propositions to chart the best course from point to A to point B. The Type II mental map depicts the *logical* organization, one capable of understanding and, to some extent, predicting the many influences in its internal and external environments.

These two governing modes seem like a compelling version of governance. Boards set goals in the strategic mode and ensure the organization reaches them in the fiduciary mode. But the mental maps underlying these two modes that suggest this governing picture is not complete. Organizations are not merely the sum of their productive and logical aspects. And if there is more to organizations, then there may be more to governing.

A more comprehensive map of the modern nonprofit organization calls for generative, Type III governing. The Type III mental map depicts the *expressive* aspects of organizations, where people are concerned not with productivity or logic alone, but also with values, judgments, and insights. But given all the hard pressures they face in ensuring accountability and supporting performance, why should boards worry about these soft aspects of organizations? Because, in short, Type III work shapes Type I and II work. Before they use various forms of managerial expertise to solve problems, organizations need to figure out which problems need solving. Before they figure out the best strategy for getting from the present to a preferred future, organizations need to figure out what that preferred future is. Before they can dedicate resources to the things they consider important, they have to figure out what things are important.

All organizations use some process or another to resolve these profoundly important issues. In the most dysfunctional organizations, these issues are settled through raw power contests and the shifting coalitions of politics. In passive organizations, they are dictated entirely by outsiders: funders, government policy makers, consumers, competitors, or accrediting organizations. In strong organizations, gifted leaders facilitate consensus on these issues. We propose that in well-governed organizations, these issues are determined by boards that work in Type III or generative mode. They are settled by boards that practice governance as leadership.

Governance as leadership entails more than working in the generative mode. Like the executive leadership so valued in organizations today, it involves not just mastering each of the governing modes, but choosing governing modes in the first place, determining when to operate in which mode. Governance as leadership, then, is a complex activity, one that cannot possibly be practiced through reliance on prescribed tasks alone.

This complexity is precisely what will worry many board observers. Isn't governing in three modes too much for boards? To the contrary. We maintain that governing-by-mode is not only more effective than governing-by-task, but that it is more engaging and meaningful. By making governing more challenging and consequential, it addresses the problem of purpose. The psychologist Mihaly Csikszentmihalyi (2003) makes a similar point about any well-constructed job. Good work, he says, relies on a "balance between opportunity and capacity." If the opportunity at hand is too challenging, it produces anxiety. If the work at hand is too easy, it produces boredom. The preferred work state—what he calls "flow"—produces concentration, absorption, and high performance because "both challenges and skills are high and equal to each other." In this sense, governance as leadership is not a burden but an opportunity.

CHAPTER 3

Type I Governing: Fiduciary

Fiduciary work is so basic to governing that most nonprofit trustees and executives consider it synonymous with trusteeship. And, lest anyone doubt the importance of fiduciary work, every few years central casting supplies a new rogue, with a new travesty, to underscore the point yet again. In 1990, Reverend Bruce Ritter was forced to resign as director of Covenant House after repeated accusations of sexual and financial misconduct. In 1992, William Aramony resigned as president of the United Way of America in the face of charges of financial mismanagement and self-dealing. In 1998, the trustees of Allegheny Health, Education and Research Foundation, in an ensemble performance, used over $20 million in endowment funds and other restricted assets for operational purposes. In 2003, the Nature Conservancy engaged in what many considered improper transactions with trustees and other supporters.

The various sins of omission and commission by for-profit boards stir further anxiety among nonprofit trustees. Tyco, WorldCom, and Enron, among others, have wreaked more damage to governance and boards of directors, more brazenly and more ingeniously, than any nonprofit. And although federal legislation in the aftermath of the scandals was aimed at public companies, the expectation quickly grew that, as a matter of best practice, nonprofits should adhere to the spirit and, to some extent, the letter of legal reforms like the Sarbanes-Oxley Act of 2002.

When these fiduciary alarms sound, nonprofits respond like most individuals faced with an emergency: reflexively. For most of us, no matter how often we have been lectured about the physics of steering into a skid, when we hit the ice, we wrench the wheel in the direction we want to go. For the nonprofit sector, the reflexive response to icy fiduciary roads has been to build and strengthen Type I boards—on the long-held assumption that fiduciary boards deliver the best governance.

In this chapter, we revisit the basic work of fiduciary governing. We consider the Type I governing that all organizations need and the Type I board that most organizations *think* they need. And by examining the mental map underlying that Type I board, we see why there is more to governing than Type I and why there is more to Type I governing than Type I boards typically offer.

TYPE I GOVERNING

Along with every other commentator on the nonprofit sector, we endorse what Type I governing aims to do: prevent theft, waste, or misuse of resources; ensure that resources are deployed effectively and efficiently to advance the organization's mission; safeguard the mission against both unintentional drift and unauthorized shifts in purpose; and require that trustees operate solely in the best interests of the organization. Together, this attention to financial discipline, informed oversight, mission fidelity, and primacy of organizational interests are recognized in the law as the board's *duties of loyalty and care.* It is the fundamental work of trusteeship.

Because these goals are familiar, they are taken for granted until a crisis occurs. But trustees need to remember that these goals constitute not only urgent legal imperatives but moral and practical imperatives as well. No nonprofit serves its cause or its constituents well by compromising on fiduciary matters. And pragmatically, no nonprofit that needs to attract clients and supporters can afford such lapses. The provision of educational, medical, or social services constitutes what economists call "credence goods." Because clients are unable to judge the quality and efficacy of services, they have to trust the integrity of the organization. People seek nonprofit hospitals that are trustworthy, not just proficient, and colleges where degrees are earned, not just purchased.

The term "trustee"[1] denotes a person who holds assets for the benefit of another. In nonprofit organizations, a board holds assets in trust for society at large or for a particular subset—for example, children at risk, art lovers or members of a given religious denomination. To serve these beneficiaries, boards typically focus on three elements of Type I work. First, they ensure that the organization's assets—especially tangible assets—are conserved and optimized to promote the organization's mission. This work typically involves oversight of audits, budgets, investments, compensation, facilities, fundraising, and executive performance and enactment of policies and practices that dis-

---

[1]The terms "board of directors" and "trustees," although used interchangeably in colloquial speech, have important legal distinctions. Trustees are generally subject to a more exacting standard in executing their duties than directors are. In most states, most boards of 501(c)(3) nonprofit organizations today would be subject to the somewhat lower directors' standard. For a full discussion of the difference, and a critique of the wider use of the directors' standard, see Fremont-Smith, 2004.

courage waste, prevent abuse, or promote efficiency. Second, boards aim to ensure that resources are used *effectively* in service of the mission. Toward this end, good boards ask not just *whether* but also *how effectively* programs advance the mission, a type of analysis that involves performance measurement. Third, boards attempt to promote lawful and ethical behavior. They seek to ensure compliance with basic standards of safety, legality, and honesty. Finally, trustees are expected to serve the interests of the organization, not self-interest. Trustees are obligated to eschew even the appearance of conflicts of interest, which may include direct or indirect financial benefits as well as relationships with competing organizations. Whether the work at hand is about efficiency, effectiveness, or ethics, most boards conduct Type I work through oversight. They routinely examine financial and programmatic reports, often through a familiar committee structure.

But good trustees also take advantage of the leadership opportunities that fiduciary work offers. In addition to the routine review essential to accountability, they also spot and debate the fiduciary significance of issues. Consider the CEO of a youth-serving organization who expected quick approval of a balanced budget proudly presented to the board. Instead, the budget prompted trustees to discuss the declining condition of the organization's recreational facilities and the low salaries and meager benefits package for staff. The board pointed out that the operating budget was, in effect, balanced on the back of the organization's facilities and personnel. After further deliberation, the board and staff decided to reconfigure an expensive but apparently ineffective program for middle-school students and to undertake a capital campaign.

Fiduciary work also reveals questions about the fit of programs and mission, providing another leadership opportunity for boards. For example, a museum director recommended an expansion of educational programs, complete with a new position of director of museum education, outreach to local schools, and an extensive Saturday art-school program for area children. She explained that the expansion could be funded by reallocating resources from other activities. In response, the board requested a more detailed cost analysis, evidence from the field of the value of these programs relative to other priorities, and an evaluation process to judge the results of the effort. This board viewed a balanced budget as only one part of its fiduciary responsibility. Program effectiveness, impact, and opportunity costs were important, too.

Exhibit 3.1 illustrates the differences between traditional fiduciary oversight and what we might call "fiduciary inquiry," which extracts leadership value from a board's engagement in fiduciary work.

Although only a brief sketch of Type I governing, this account is doubtless familiar to most trustees. Trustees know why it is indispensable and, on the whole, they know how to provide fiduciary oversight, if only in the narrowest sense of the term. Society wants more Type I governing, practiced more diligently. Much less is known, however, about the organizational assumptions that underlie Type I. We turn now to the perspectives on organizations that shape Type I governing. This mental map helps answer important questions: What must people assume about organizations if this is the way they govern them? What kind of organization, or what aspect of organizations, is best suited to Type I governing?

| EXHIBIT 3.1 | FIDUCIARY OVERSIGHT TO FIDUCIARY INQUIRY |

Fiduciary Oversight Questions	Fiduciary Inquiry Questions
Can we afford it?	What's the opportunity cost?
Did we get a clean audit?	What can we learn from the audit?
Is the budget balanced?	Does the budget reflect our priorities?
Should we increase departmental budgets by 2%—or 3%?	Should we move resources from one program to another?
Will the proposed program attract enough clients?	How will the program advance our mission?
Does a merger make financial sense?	Does a merger make mission sense?
Is it legal?	Is it ethical?
How much money do we need to raise?	What's the case for raising the money?
Can we secure the gift?	How will the gift advance our mission? Does the donor expect too much control?
Is staff turnover reasonable?	Are we treating staff fairly and respectfully?

THE TYPE I MENTAL MAP

The familiar arrangements of Type I governing—the division of labor among committees (budget, audit, endowment, and so on), the routine production and review of technical reports, and highly structured board meetings with fixed agendas and parliamentary rules—are all outgrowths of what may be the most innovative and enduring organizational form ever envisioned: the bureaucracy.

Early twentieth-century giants of organizational and sociological theory, notably Max Weber and Frederick W. Taylor, developed theories of leadership and organization that helped society respond to the profound changes wrought by the Industrial Revolution. Where previously an individual artisan designed and created a product from start to finish, the emergence of the assembly line allowed essentially unskilled workers to learn and perform repetitively one small step of the production process which, in turn, enabled the mass production of standardized goods (Scott, 2003).

The artisan's workshop was suddenly irrelevant. Weber's theory of bureaucracy helped large industrial collectives cope with the new challenge of coordination. He introduced a raft of ideas that promised organizational effectiveness and efficiency at all levels and that are still fundamental to our conception of an organization. These include precise division of labor, novel in an age when assignments were made at will by leaders; hierarchy of offices, which limited the authority of any one person; and fixed rules to govern performance, as opposed to rules that could be changed at the leader's whim (Scott, 2003).

Hand in hand with bureaucracy, and also central to Type I governing, is another construct so familiar that it is hidden in plain sight: the idea of principal–agent accountability. Perhaps more than any other, this unglamorous idea makes capitalism possible. It allows for the duties of owners and managers to be neatly divided, so that an owner (the principal) can hire a manager (the agent) to run the organization. The owner tries to ensure that the agent acts on behalf of the principal. Instead of managing the firm, the principal *oversees* the *agent's* management of the firm, in much the same way that a board oversees a CEO. Though nonprofits are ownerless by definition, the parallels to for-profit organizations make the principal–agent construct relevant. Along with the idea of bureaucracy, the principal–agent model continues to animate much of the Type I governing practiced today.

There is a good reason that the basic conventions of the Type I board—a CEO and board meeting in isolation around a table in the organization's conference room with only an occasional outsider present—are so prevalent. Type I governing sees organizations largely as closed systems, free to set and pursue goals without regard to environmental forces. The board looks inward to check for trouble and outward largely for financial purposes. If the organization has an endowment to manage, trustees pay attention to the impact of financial markets on organizational assets or, in the absence of an endowment, to the impact of the larger economy on fundraising and revenue generation. But most Type I board business takes place within the confines of the organization. This is where agents in service to principals can best be observed.

In short, Weber would certainly admire modern attempts to clarify the roles and responsibilities of boards, to codify the separation of power between boards and executives, and to convert the obligations of fiduciary duty into a series of manageable, discrete, committee-driven processes. It is no surprise, then, that boards function like industrial quality-inspectors, walking the factory floor to be sure that defects are detected and corrected, and that wayward workers do not misuse resources.

Surely this is no one's vision of an organization today, but it is the cluster of assumptions underlying Type I governing. In fact, the bureaucratic assumptions of Type I governing have become institutionalized in the *Type I board*, a problematic archetype even for the fiduciary goals this model was designed to advance.

THE TYPE I BOARD

The Type I board is a bundle of Type I governing practices set in concrete. The fiduciary work of budgeting, auditing, investment management, development, and program review became a series of fixed committees, one for each production process of the organization. The protocol of oversight became a basic template for board agendas: Listen passively to reports and occasionally ask questions of management. Rules of parliamentary procedure shaped board discourse. Even the profile of Type I board members became standardized: people with technical expertise or managerial competence were appointed, the better to oversee management and do the technical work of fiduciary governing. More than many modern organizations, the Type I board looks like a slice of the bureaucratic organization of the early twentieth century, when workers repetitively and dutifully performed assigned tasks.

Although not all boards conform to this classic design, there is ample incentive to do so. It is important not only for boards to do fiduciary work, but to be seen doing it as well. Symbolically, the Type I board provides constituents with assurances of organizational integrity which, in turn, help attract money, clients, staff, and goodwill. But this legitimacy comes at a price when Type I governing institutionalizes four flawed assumptions about organizations.

Nonprofits may have bureaucratic features, but they are not bureaucracies. Nonprofits are not bureaucracies per se, and none wish to be. Like other organizations, nonprofits have bureaucratic features that serve useful purposes. Evidence of bureaucracy can be observed in organizational charts, position descriptions, staff handbooks, constitutions, bylaws, labor contracts, and other formal documents that delineate responsibilities and designate approved work procedures. Many organizational functions, such as payroll, accounting, purchasing, and government reporting require worker training, standardization of procedures, and clear chains of command.

These bureaucratic features are eminently functional. Without them, organizations would be in constant chaos, disputing, negotiating, and reinventing each day the basic rules and procedures by which the staff and board operate. Modern society views bureaucracies as sclerotic or obsolete largely because it no longer remembers what came before. "Because obedience is owed not to a person—whether a traditional chief or a charismatic leader—but to a set of impersonal principles," wrote organizational theorist W. Richard Scott, "subordinates in bureaucratic systems have firmer grounds for independent action, guided by their interpretation of the principles. They also have a clear basis for questioning the direction of superiors, whose actions are presumably constrained by the same impersonal framework of rules" (2003). Bureaucracy may be a problem, but anarchy would be a bigger one.

The weakness of the Type I mental map is that it describes *only* the bureaucratic dimensions of organizations, and this is too restricted a construct to explain how modern nonprofits actually operate. Beyond the institutionalized aspects of an organization are the informal dimensions, which are no less real than the policy manual. This uncharted organization consists of constituent views, political dynamics, human relations, and social interactions both within the organization and between the organization and its environment. These forces conflict with one another, disrupt chains of command, undercut standard operating procedures, and undo the rational plans and expectations of board and management. Real organizations, then, are more than the rational theorist's instrument for goal attainment. They have their structural aspects, but they are not bureaucracies.

Many leaders are agents in name only. The Type I board imagines the board and CEO in a principal–agent relationship. But increasingly the chief executive acts as the leader of the organization. Indeed, no one gains entry to society's pantheon of organizational leaders as someone's agent. For example, we do not remember Andrew Carnegie, John D. Rockefeller, or Henry Ford as agents, nor did they act like agents. Even the rise of complex organizations has not displaced the heroic leader. Alfred P. Sloan, the legendary CEO of General Motors, for example, championed now ubiquitous organizational tools like written plans, committees, and multidivisional structures precisely because he knew a single leader was no match for a complex organization. Ironically, Sloan's attempts to shift attention away from personal leadership to organizational systems helped establish his reputation as a leader of singular brilliance. And today it is difficult to imagine Jack Welch, late of General Electric, or Lou Gerstner, former chief of IBM, as agents of their boards.

Even in the nonprofit sector—ground zero for the mobilization of collective action—leaders reign more and more. The move away from the dowdy title of "executive director" (an avatar of principal–agent) to "chief executive officer" speaks to a trend, as does the advent of the "social entrepreneur," a visionary who delivers innovations to society. A few nonprofit leaders rank with the industry giants, at least for a time, in public consciousness. Think of Frances Hesselbein, former president of the Girl Scouts USA, whose reputation for leadership landed her on the cover of *Business Week,* under the (somewhat patronizing) title "Surprise! Some of America's best-run organizations are nonprofits" ("Learning from Nonprofits," 1990). Legendary university presidents like Theodore Hesburgh of Notre Dame and James Conant of Harvard were powerful, rarely challenged leaders. These celebrated chief executives, we suspect, hardly had a self-image as agents of their boards.

Boards are principals mostly in name. If the idea of CEO as agent is implausible, so too is the idea of a board as a principal directing its agent. Most people tend to think of leadership as singular, not plural. Howard Gardner, who plowed new ground with the idea of multiple intelligence, reflects this still dominant view, defining a leader as "an individual (or, *rarely,* a set of individuals) who significantly affects the thoughts, feelings, and/or behaviors of a significant number of individuals" (H. Gardner, in collaboration with Emma Laskin, 1995, emphasis added).

Amidst all this admiration for the larger-than-life leader comes the Type I board, wedded to the theory that boards are principals and CEOs are agents. In reality, most Type I boards accept and even promote the idea of the chief executive as a heroic leader. Most cite the selection of the CEO as, by far, the single most important decision the board ever makes. Board members regularly boast about their powerful, decisive, visionary chief executive.

If trustees have any qualms about their own importance to the organization, they take comfort in their nominal role as policy maker. Of course, as so often happens, the CEO actually decides what policies to present for the board's approval. Boards do exercise the power of principals at rare intervals, typically at times of leadership transition or crisis. Much of the rest of the time, boards are merely watching, not directing, the CEO. If too much trouble occurs too often, the board may be compelled to change CEOs. More often, it is powerful agents who direct passive principals.

Organizations are not closed systems. While most trustees understand intuitively that organizations are susceptible to environmental influence, the Type I board expects to focus on internal issues (except for fundraising and investing), thereby discouraging trustee engagement in the boundary-spanning work crucial to the success of nonprofit organizations. Type I boards have traditionally assumed that mission-driven organizations are somehow insulated from external forces. Some, at great peril, have chosen to disregard environmental cues and navigate only by an internal compass, ignoring client preferences, competitive forces, alternative providers, expectations of funders, and changes in technology. Other Type I boards have taken a broader view. Yet when these boards do look outward, through strategic planning, for example, it is most often at a special meeting or off-site retreat. Strategic work simply does not fit the routines of Type I boards.

We started by affirming the aims and centrality of fiduciary governing. Type I governing does not pose problems. Type I boards do.

ASSESSING THE PROBLEMS

The Type I board creates three problems: too much Type I governing; too few leadership opportunities for boards; and too many symptoms of the substitute's dilemma.

Type I all the time. Type I boards encourage Type I governing above all else and at all times. Boards can and do govern in other modes—but often despite their Type I board assumptions. Think of the preparations that many boards need in order to discuss organizational strategy—one of the key duties of the modern board. Extra meetings are scheduled because the typical board meeting is so short, crowded, and carefully orchestrated. The venue changes, along with board members' attire. The session often starts with exercises that enable more productive interpersonal dynamics. Robert's Rules of Order are out of order, replaced by a facilitator to guide the board through an inquisitive, inclusive, spontaneous conversation.

When strategic planning needs to be integrated into ongoing board deliberations, the problem is subtler. The problem is not the Type I edifice, but rather the type of thinking it promotes: technical, incremental, and intended mostly to detect and correct errors. It is suitable for dealing piecemeal with slivers of complex organizations, rather than synthesizing disparate elements to understand the whole. It is a type of thinking that makes the boardroom look like a back office, where middle-level workers pore over data-filled reports to keep the train on track. It is a thought process associated with bureaucratic bean counters, not organizational leaders.

At worst, Type I board members are like students drilled to recite facts, rather than grasp concepts and principles, in order to pass a high-stakes test, or like attorneys who can cite from memory the rules of evidence but lack the skills to cross-examine a witness or sway a jury. The rote work that produces a high test score or thorough recall of the law provides little advantage when the issue at hand requires creativity and intellectual agility. Whether trustee, CEO, litigator, or student, performance suffers when one cannot escape a mode that serves well for technical tasks but impedes more complicated and nuanced work.

Type I boards limit leadership opportunities. The Type I board marginalizes the best of Type I governing. Oversight displaces inquiry. Inherently rich questions of organizational purpose and performance are reduced to an exercise in Management 101, even at large or elite institutions with sophisticated trustees. For example, the Type I board of a museum would explore a proposed new wing solely as a matter of cost and a component of a capital campaign. On the other hand, a true fiduciary would examine the relationship of the addition to the museum's goal of becoming an educational resource as well as an exhibition space—which may be more consequential consideration for the museum's long-term vitality. Similarly, a Type I college board presented with a slate of candidates for tenure might ask about the budgetary implications of the recommended appointments but not inquire about the fit between the faculty's expertise and the institution's strategic goals. In both cases, the board's financial blinders obscure important questions.

Presented with an agenda, a Type I board proceeds reflexively, as if the goal were to complete a governance punch list. Discussions are brief, often perfunctory; committee and board votes are mechanical and pro forma. Dissent has no place. A good board does not get "side-tracked" or fall behind schedule.

The typical agenda of a Type I board indicates how a group of intelligent people can be consumed by fiduciary tasks. Agendas are, of course, artifacts of bureaucracy designed to control and organize discussions that might otherwise meander unproductively. Imperfect as they are, agendas are valued precisely for this reason. But leadership creates value by *interrupting* such routine. A finance or facilities committee might have to approve a contract to repair a roof; however an entire agenda of routine matters all but guarantees that the board will add marginal value at best. A more consequential topic might be the larger question of deferred maintenance, unfunded depreciation, or the challenge of intergenerational equity—the trade-off between funding today's needs and tomorrow's. Exhibit 3.2 offers some illustrative questions that invite boards to explore the deeper implications of fiduciary issues that often lie just beneath the surface.

EXHIBIT 3.2	REFLECTIONS ON FIDUCIARY ISSUES

- What do we hold in trust, and for whom?
- What are the fiduciary, but nonfinancial, roles of our board and committees?
- How do we know the organization is fulfilling its mission?
- Does a proposed initiative effectively advance our mission?
- What safeguards do we have in place to avoid the well-publicized fiduciary failure of some other nonprofit board?
- If we held an annual stakeholders' meeting, what would we say about the organization's fiduciary performance and the board's effectiveness as a steward?
- What is the evidence that we are a trustworthy organization? What are some examples of times when we earned the title of "trustworthy?"
- What are our major financial vulnerabilities? What are we doing as an organization and a board to address them?
- Even though we are not obligated to abide by Sarbanes-Oxley and similar legislation, should we voluntarily adopt certain principles and practices these laws require?

The substitute's dilemma. To the extent that boards institutionalize bureaucratic approaches to governing, trustees will become vulnerable to the fatigue and boredom of highly routinized work, and the fiduciary value that the Type I boards are engineered to produce will be jeopardized.

These problems challenge trustees to think about reflexive responses to the obligations of fiduciary governing. Can they identify and exploit the leadership opportunities that Type I work presents—finding and framing fiduciary challenges? Perhaps more important, can boards, in effect, learn to steer into a skid? Can trustees do fiduciary governing, as they must, without freezing in the form of a fiduciary board? Can they practice other types of governing, not as a substitute for fiduciary work, but as a complement to it?

CONCLUSION

Type I *governance* is essential, but the Type I *board* is problematic. First, the urgent drives out the important, and the stress on efficiency displaces the quest for effectiveness. Second, the board adds value primarily to the technical core of the organization, not to the core purposes of the organization. Third, the board's work becomes so predictable and perfunctory as to be tedious and monotonous. Trustees become bored spectators at a dull event. Worst of all, the routines of the Type I board become so deeply ingrained that the board cannot see the larger picture or govern in another mode. Every issue looks like a fiduciary matter, and every trustee thinks only like a fiduciary. The more the board behaves in this manner, the more management obliges with exclusively fiduciary agendas supported by exclusively fiduciary information. Before long, the board develops such a limited sense of the organization that the trustees' ability to challenge and enrich organizational thinking atrophies.

CHAPTER 4

Type II Governing: Strategic

If the standards of success for nonprofits were purely legal compliance and financial equilibrium, then Type I boards might suffice. But just as healthy and prosperous people also seek purpose, connection, and fulfillment, nonprofits—*especially* nonprofits—have comparable needs: the desire to serve a socially valuable mission, to have a positive impact, and to create communities of interest. For these reasons, nonprofits need strategy.

To participate in strategic governance, trustees need a new mental map that goes beyond Type I terrain, where organizations are machine-like bureaucracies, chief executives are managers who implement board decisions, and organizations are insulated from the influence of constituents and the larger environment. A Type II mental map charts new territory, where organizations are complex human systems, chief executives are leaders (though neither omniscient nor omnipotent), and nonprofits are highly permeable organizations susceptible to both internal and external influence.

Guided by a Type II map, the board's attention shifts from conformance toward performance, and the trustees' perspective changes from "inside out" to "outside in." Balanced budgets are no longer sufficient if resources are dedicated to the wrong purposes; lawful conduct has only nominal value if the organization serves no useful social purpose. In Type II governance, an organization seeks to align internal strengths and weaknesses with external opportunities and threats, all in pursuit of organizational impact.

Trustees must cope with an additional challenge in Type II governance: a barrage of organizational theory, prescription, advice, and gimmickry that offers scores of ways to understand and influence strategy. To complicate the problem, most of these treatises are aimed primarily at for-profit executives. Partly as a result, many nonprofit boards attempt to do Type II work with a Type I mindset and tool kit that foster formal strategic planning—important work for organizations but not for trustees. To govern strategically, boards need to think, not plan, strategically. To help understand the difference, we trace briefly how these two approaches to strategy have evolved and influenced, if not confounded, trustees.

NONPROFITS ENTER THE MARKETPLACE

Considerations of strategy have permeated discussions of corporate performance since the 1970s. Hundreds, if not thousands, of authors and consultants have suggested (or guaranteed) how companies can gain competitive advantage, either quickly or over the long run. As strategy became fashionable among corporations, most nonprofits continued to act as if the sector enjoyed a grant of immunity from competitive and environmental forces. The dominant "theory" was that success depended more on the organization's self-evident virtues and unique purposes than on a carefully crafted strategy. Financial support was an act of faith and charity, not a response to an inspired strategy. Then circumstances changed.

- Demand for the services of some nonprofits declined. For instance, private colleges and universities confronted stiff competition from lower-priced public institutions. And with cutbacks in insurance reimbursements and the growth of outpatient treatment, hospitals were saddled with empty beds and budget deficits.

- Arts organizations, from orchestras to museums to ballet companies, simultaneously encountered a bevy of challenges: resistance to expensive tickets, distaste for modern genres, unfavorable demographics, and intense competition from popular culture for the attention of younger audiences.

- Nonprofits became subject to external ratings such as *US News & World Report*'s rankings of colleges, Leap Frog's assessments of hospitals, and GuideStar's financial analyses of charities. The comparative data enlightened and empowered consumers, shaped public perceptions, and prodded administrators to be responsive to customer concerns.

- Government agencies, foundations, and philanthropists started to treat grants to nonprofit organizations more like investments than gifts. Resource providers wanted objective assurances that allocations to a particular organization would yield a higher rate of social return than an alternative investment opportunity.

- With more information available about nonprofits' performance, competition for personnel intensified as well. A high-performing organization could attract better staff and trustees than a low-rated one. Who wouldn't rather be associated with a frontrunner than an also-ran?

Eventually, nonprofit organizations realized that these profound changes in the environment could no longer be ignored.

Strategy became an essential organizational focus, and the board became a player. Steeped in strategy at work, many trustees were eager and able to apply these same techniques to nonprofits.

BOARDS AND FORMAL STRATEGY: A TYPE I APPROACH TO TYPE II WORK

Strategy has now become a watchword, if not a mantra, for the not-for-profit sector. The mere adoption of a strategic plan (never mind successful implementation) suggests, *ipso facto,* organizational professionalism and legitimacy. Few nonprofits can afford to be without a written plan. Funders and other influential constituencies expect a strategic plan no less than a budget and an audit. Savvy prospective trustees ask to see the plan which, at least symbolically, signifies professional management and organizational maturity. Normally, a few leaders of the organization, sometimes aided by consultants with off-the-shelf tools and step-by-step techniques, create or guide the development of *the* plan, a formal document often adorned with four-color graphics.

Like immigrants to a new land, many trustees import old customs to a new world; they carry the baggage of bureaucracy to the realm of strategy. The first and natural inclination of trustees is to do strategy the old way, much as boards do finance, facilities, and programs. Just as boards required and reviewed budgets, boards now expect to approve plans and monitor implementation. In fact, boards treat budgets and plans rather similarly. The standard procedure is to ask technical questions: Do we have the money, the space, the personnel? Do we have a feasible time line? Are the demographic or inflationary projections reasonable? Have we included benchmarks and milestones? Consistent with the view that organizational leaders bear responsibility for crafting strategy, trustees generally accept the substance of the plan with only minor modifications. Even more to the point, the plan often reaches the board with the most consequential considerations already rationalized and resolved. Alternative scenarios and the downside risks of staff recommendations are either omitted or addressed summarily.

Type I boards follow the precept that "A board does not formulate strategy; its function is review" (Andrews, 1971). In this spirit, fiduciary boards attempt to do Type II work in Type I mode. Trustees approve the strategic plan and monitor implementation, usually based on written and oral reports from management. The board's primary role is to ensure that the chief executive has developed and installed a comprehensible, defensible plan. Once the board approves the plan, trustees sometimes serve on committees and task forces directed to execute various aspects of the plan, especially initiatives related to finances and facilities.

As strategy evolved, so too has the board's role, sparked by a new emphasis on competitive position, a concept pioneered by Harvard Business School professor Michael Porter. In an article that asked, "What Is Strategy?," Porter (1996) answered, "Strategic positioning means performing *different* activities from rivals' or performing similar activities in *different* ways." Influenced by the fundamental message of *Competitive Strategy,* the title of Porter's landmark book (1980), more sophisticated boards pose questions quite different from the more technically oriented Type I line of inquiry. For instance, trustees now ask: What business are we in? What do our customers want? Where do we have a comparative advantage? What are our core competencies? Some nonprofit CEOs and staff are unsettled by these questions, which clearly imply that competition is real, that missions cannot be disentangled from markets, that nonprofits have to be selective and strategic about priorities and, perhaps most uncomfortably, that organizations have to change in order to succeed. While some staff may prefer to imagine a glorious future, oblivious to troublesome truths, few have that luxury.

STRATEGIC DISILLUSIONMENT

Practical experience has not always produced the dramatic results touted by proponents of formal planning. Like other instant solutions and managerial panaceas, such as Zero-Based Budgeting, Total Quality Management, and Business Process Reengineering, the virtues of planning have been oversold and the drawbacks overlooked (Shapiro, 1995). Gradually, the pendulum swung in the other direction. Birnbaum (2000) described this stage as "narrative devolution," a period when "overly optimistic claims of success are replaced by overly pessimistic claims that the signs of disappointment are everywhere..."

Enter Henry Mintzberg. More than anyone else, Mintzberg is the naysayer of formal strategic planning, as reflected by the title of his authoritative work, *The Rise and Fall of Strategic Planning* (1994). Mintzberg argued that formal planning was overly reliant on hyper-rational analysis to achieve expressed goals. The lockstep mechanics of the process and the press to develop a logical, linear game plan squelched creativity and synthesis, the necessary catalysts for new ideas to blossom. Inventiveness and resourcefulness, Mintzberg asserted, cannot be programmed into a planning process, as if " 'be creative' or 'think boldly' [can be] an isolated step, another box on a chart." Quoting organizational theorist Karl Weick, Mintzberg continued, "Scientific

thinking is probably a poor model for managerial thinking..."
The "grand fallacy" of formal strategic planning, he concluded,
was that, "Because analysis is not synthesis, strategic planning
is not strategy formation." While few people would explain the
problem in these terms, disillusionment with strategic planning
has escalated. The plans of nonprofit organizations (and some
corporations, too) frequently seem to be the triumph of a cum-
bersome process over progress. Sometimes, the actual weight of
the plan seems greater than its substantive heft.

For many nonprofit boards that have embraced formal strategic planning, one overarching concern has arisen: the organization's strategic plan is neither strategic nor a plan. A swirl of six
different, yet related, problems contributes to the sense among
many trustees that the strategic plans of nonprofits are more
utopian portraits than blueprints for action.

1. *Plans without traction.* A formal plan, in theory, details how an
organization expects to move from current circumstances to a
preferred state. The process usually involves extrapolations from
the present to the future. However, nonprofits normally accord
far more attention to the latter than the former. And therein lies
the rub. In many plans, dreams trump realities. There are pages
upon pages devoted to a brighter future with little or no
attention to current conditions or the perhaps inconveniently
intractable financial, political, and cultural realities that impede
or preclude notable progress. The "blue-sky" quality of these
plans overshadows down-to-earth considerations—the practical
yet crucial daily routines that must change to realize a new
vision. As a result, the status quo, ironically, goes relatively
unchallenged and unchanged except incrementally, the very
approach strategic plans are supposedly designed to avert. As a

former university president once quipped, "The status quo is the only condition the faculty cannot veto." In fact, formal plans, quite inadvertently, tend to consolidate the status quo and trigger expectations among staff that *more* resources would be allocated to better support the grander ambitions of current programs (Schmidtlein, 1988). To the extent that trustees expected significant change or even an overhaul of the organization's business model, disappointment was almost inevitable.

2. *Plans without patterns.* The discipline of formal strategic planning requires that decisions and activities be tightly integrated in order to achieve desired goals. As Andrews (1971) and many other strategists stressed, there must be a *pattern* of decisions and actions. People, policies, programs, budgets, incentives, and facilities must be harmonized with the plan. Each part reinforces the other. Yet, few formal nonprofit plans specify the changes in organizational architecture and procedures required to realize an espoused strategy. Instead, the plans assume that the current organizational structures, reward systems, budget processes, and production functions will more or less suffice. The plans, perhaps naively, presume that institutions can somehow be repositioned on the outside with few or no substantial changes on the inside—an approach that skeptics dub "planning by wishful thinking." Under these conditions, trustees are baffled by the disconnect between rhetorical ambitions and administrative processes.

3. *Plans without strategies.* The formal plans of many nonprofits have a paradoxical quality: specific goals and a vague strategy. Too often, nonprofit plans (and we have read many) proclaim a vision, for instance, that the college will be the best of breed,

that the hospital will provide the best health care in the region, or that the museum will be cited as the most innovative arts institution in the state. Specific objectives may be to attract more and better clients, to develop a stronger reputation in the community, to enlarge the endowment, to earn more revenue, or to recruit more capable staff. *What* will produce these outcomes, and *what* will create competitive advantage and neutralize threats—beyond the proverbial creation of task forces to pursue these very questions—remains unstated or underdeveloped. It is as if a corporation's strategy were to double sales with no mention of new products or services. In the absence of "strategic drivers," the competitively advantageous and organizationally appropriate ideas that actually propel a plan, many board members worry that there is no "there" there—and perhaps little reason to be there as trustees, either.

4. *Ideas without input.* Sometimes, a plan does, in fact, include a few "big ideas" or bold departures from the status quo. More often than not, however, these "proposals" reach the boardroom as prepackaged recommendations from the chief executive, prenegotiated with the professional staff. The inclusive nature of the process to this point produces a consensus that CEOs are understandably loath to have boards undo or amend. At that juncture, trustees are invited to plan, not to strategize—to provide assistance, as needed and requested by management, to *implement* a strategy predicated on the ideas of others. Cognizant of these patterns, some trustees begin to wonder why disenfranchisement starts at the top of the organization chart, and CEOs start to wonder why trustee disengagement seems to accelerate after ratification of the plan.

5. *The pace of change.* To no small degree, faith in formal strategy stands on a conviction that bright people can correctly predict the future without being surprised. And, indeed, there are aspects of the future that are foreseeable for planning purposes. This year's enrollment, patient count, or concert subscriptions usually presage next year's. The budget, as a rule, does not vary much from year to year. Employee turnover can be reasonably predicted, based on historical data, in stable organizations. Such elements of predictability can tempt (or delude) trustees to think that top-notch executives have an unobstructed view of the future.

Yet, unanticipated events can make plans irrelevant. The CEO accepts a position elsewhere, a competitor introduces a better idea, a major gift fails to materialize, a scandal erupts, the value of the endowment declines, or constituents simply resist change. The further ahead a plan reaches, the less likely its assumptions will endure. In an often turbulent and interdependent environment, nonprofit executives sometimes can barely see five days, let alone five years, into the future.

Under these circumstances, trustees, like others in the organization, become disillusioned. The more effort board members expend on formal long-range plans, the greater the prospects for disappointment. Board members start to notice that large portions of the formal plan rapidly become inoperative and that key elements of the enacted strategy are actually unplanned. Enthusiasm for the process diminishes as plans become outdated or, worse, shelved.

6. *Unforeseen outcomes.* The formal approach to strategy also assumes that skillful managers can predict the future outcomes

of present actions. Boards traditionally prize (and believe) a chief executive confident enough to assure that planned initiatives will produce intended results. While an assembly line can be programmed to manufacture a uniform product, the processes of nonprofit organizations are more mysterious and less controllable. An organization may, for example, develop a new program, based on the best available research to prevent teenage pregnancy. However, certain characteristics of the organization's target population may confound the premises of the program, changes in government funding may undermine success, or staff may execute ineffectively.

Meanwhile, something else, not even mentioned in the plan, succeeds beyond anyone's expectations. In fact, the trustees may be unaware of the program until *after* a level of conspicuous success has been attained. If the success occurs at a low enough level of a relatively large organization, even the chief executive may be surprised. Trustees eager to know what is really going on in the organization, what is working and what is not, realize (usually sooner than later) that the strategic plan is not always the best place to look.

Despite these six obstacles, formal plans have important positive effects. As we stated earlier, strategic plans are badges of legitimacy. No nonprofit wants to be "illegitimate" and no chief executive wants to appear unprofessional. Formal, written plans safeguard against both risks. The standard cycle—plan, implement, assess, adjust, and plan anew—ensures that CEOs play a prominent role ascribed to leaders, and the well-choreographed sequence of events offers trustees a measure of comfort and confidence. In addition, and by no means inconsequential, the planning process creates "excuses" for organizations to converse internally and externally, and plans provide plausible rationales for managers to make decisions and allocate resources. As we highlight the frustrations that trustees and staff experience with formal strategic planning, we do not discount the benefits.

The central drawback of strategic planning, however, has become a near fatal flaw in the minds of many. For instance, Gary Hamel (1996), a professor of strategy and consultant to Fortune 500 companies, decried formal strategy as "ritualistic...reductionist...and elitist...harnessing only a small proportion of an organization's creative potential." For-profits and nonprofits alike were in search of a better idea and, lo and behold, *ideas* were the answer.

STRATEGIC THINKING: BEYOND A TYPE I MINDSET

Rather than rely only on a formal, analytical, and technical process detailing the sequence of steps that will move an organization to a preferred future, leaders can arrive at strategy another way: through insight, intuition, and improvisation. In a word, leaders can *think,* and strategy-as-thinking can produce "Strategy as Revolution" (Hamel 1996). Breakthrough strategies, impelled by new ideas, enable organizations to exploit new opportunities and capture new markets. According to this view, the gods are no longer in the details; the gods (and leaders) are in the clouds. Details are delegated to mere managers. Leaders are strategic thinkers, not strategic planners. The byword is "BHAGs," an acronym for big, hairy, audacious goals. (As Exhibit 4.1 illustrates, some nonprofits have, in fact, been revolutionary and, in the case of higher education, a for-profit has

EXHIBIT 4.1	"BIG HAIRY AUDACIOUS GOALS" (BHAGS) IN NONPROFIT REALMS

In health care, "focused factories" were the BHAG. Institutions like the Mayo Clinic in Rochester, Minnesota, the Cleveland Clinic, and the Shouldice Hospital in Toronto achieved excellence, efficiency, and profitability through standardization and specialization. Shouldice, in fact, does *"only* abdominal hernia operations" (Herzlinger 1997). All rejected the dominant model of a comprehensive health care center that was all cures for all people.

In religion, Willow Creek Community Church (Mellado, 1991) outside Chicago, Prestonwood Baptist Church in Plano, Texas, Southeast Christian Church in Grapevine, Texas, and several other mega-churches (Brown, 2002), merged traditional religion with market segmentation, customer orientation, and contemporary entertainment. This was done to attract thousands upon thousands of new worshipers, even as attendance dwindled at mainline congregations. So-called "full-service" churches became "one-stop shops" for prayer, recreation, food, and fellowship.

In higher education, the BHAG was the "invasion" of the University of Phoenix. In some twenty years, this *for-profit* university became the largest university in the United States, with some 250,000 students enrolled in on-site and online degree programs worldwide. Despite contemptuous criticism and bitter resistance from traditionalists, the university rewrote the rulebook, or better, *invented* a new rulebook, on how to deliver a quality university education to a mass audience. Many nonprofit universities, however reluctantly or desperately, adopted "best practices" that not only made Phoenix a phenomenon, but also made the stock, traded on NASDAQ as the Apollo Group, the second best performer on that exchange for the most current five-year period.

revolutionized the "industry.") In each of these cases, brilliant ideas, not brilliant plans, were the springboard for revolutionary strategies. Yes, execution matters, but execution by "rule-breakers," not "rule takers." The quintessential elements of strategic thinking are well-captured, by exception, in a description of strategic planning by Hamel and Prahalad (1997):

> It seldom escapes the boundaries of existing business units. It seldom illuminates new white space opportunities. It seldom uncovers the unarticulated needs of customers. It seldom provides any insight into how to rewrite industry rules. It seldom stretches to encompass the threat from nontraditional competitors. It seldom forces managers to confront their potentially out-of-date conventions. Strategic planning always starts with "what is." It seldom starts with "what could be."

Because BHAGs and breakthroughs garner most of the attention, nonprofits may conclude that strategic thinking has limited utility from day to day. This is a mistake on at least two counts. First, strategic thinking is not merely for the desperate. Even the healthiest organizations, from time to time, need to "revolutionize," the central thesis of *The Innovator's Dilemma,* Clayton Christensen's (1997) influential study, which shows how thriving businesses become indifferent to competitive threats and too entrenched to adapt. Second, the principles of strategic thinking that produce BHAGs are just as germane to organizational choices that are not nearly as spectacular. The concept applies to much more than "bet-the-company" decisions. Organizations face myriad choices replete with strategic implications. Strategic thinking should not be treated as heavy artillery or a last-ditch measure deployed only at times of crisis. It is, in fact, most useful when honed through continuous use.

As we stress strategic thinking more than strategic planning, we note an important constraint: "the bottleneck is at the top of the bottle" (Hamel, 1996). That is, senior executives are the least likely to imagine or advocate dramatic organizational changes because they have the "largest investment in the past, and the greatest reverence for industrial dogma." Therefore, one is "unlikely to find a pro-change constituency" among top managers. However, there are thinkers elsewhere in the organization, especially at the borders of the organization. "The capacity for strategic innovation increases proportionately with each mile you move away from headquarters." Since wisdom, knowledge, and experience are widely distributed in an organization, a transformative idea can spring from anywhere. Strategic thinking occurs as a democratic process, not in the sense that everyone votes and the majority wins, but rather that everyone has opportunities to champion a point of view and to exert influence based on the quality of one's ideas rather than one's place on the organization chart. Although proponents of strategic thinking never mention boards, the implications for governance are quite profound—so much so that boards of trustees must govern in a different mode.

GOVERNING IN TYPE II MODE

If formal strategy alone were sufficient to imagine and guide an organization's future, then board oversight in a fiduciary mode might be adequate. But if an organization's strategy rests on new concepts and reconsidered value propositions, and if the chief executive cannot (and should not) be the sole source of these ideas, then a board must do more than mandate and monitor a plan. The role of the board shifts, in a way, from brawn to brains, from the power of the board's oversight—whether exercised as compliance cops or forfeited as rubber stamps—to the power of the board's ideas. In Type II governance, "What do you think?," when asked of trustees, does not mean "What do you think of management's plans?" It really means "What is *your* thinking about the organization's future?"

At a distance from the executive suite, and thus relatively independent-minded, trustees meet Hamel's criteria for strategic thinkers. Equipped with extensive experience, broad intelligence, and seasoned judgment, most trustees can see (or quickly learn to see) "the big picture" and can capably discuss the "big idea." (Exhibit 4.2 provides abbreviated versions of questions that various organizations have posed to spur trustees to think beyond the technical parameters of a formal plan.)

At the same time, general intelligence alone does not ensure the best thinking. Trustees must understand the organization's basic business model and "strategic service vision," (Heskett, 1987) which includes: target markets, service concept (or the value proposition), operating strategy, and delivery system. These are domains where trustees, without the detailed knowledge staff possess, can still think strategically. In fact, as smart generalists, the board's capacity to see the panorama more clearly than the pixels underscores a central tenet of Type II governance: boards are better suited to think together than plan together, to expand the essence of a great idea rather than elaborate the details of a plan.

THE EVOLUTION OF STRATEGIC GOVERNANCE

We first proposed a strategic role for boards that is not rooted in Type I mode in *The Effective Board of Trustees* (Chait, Holland, and Taylor, 1993). In that empirical study of nonprofit governance, we concluded that one of six dimensions of board effectiveness was the strategic dimension: "a board's ability to envision and shape institutional direction." We learned that the most effective boards "cultivate and concentrate on processes

EXHIBIT 4.2   STRATEGIC THINKING
BIG PICTURE QUESTIONS

- Is the "business model" of this and other research universities viable over the next 20 years? If not, what has to change? How well-positioned are we to change?
- Do we want to be a museum that pushes the limits of free expression and societal tastes? If so, how will that affect community and government support?
- What if our customers start to view boarding schools as outdated, isolated enclaves of the elite?
- What forms of health care should we emphasize at a hospital with multiple missions (that is, teaching, research, patient care) and huge financial losses? Should we discontinue traumatic care for indigent patients?
- Can we flourish in a neighborhood in decline? If not, do we relocate? Do we ally with a community development corporation? Do we underwrite "gentrification" and subsidize staff housing?
- What is the future of academic medicine? Does this university want to own or affiliate with hospitals? To what degree should we specialize? Where do we have competitive advantage?
- What will be the consequences to this university now that others have started to make knowledge free on the web?
- How far will we go, vis-à-vis the competition, in the amenities arms race to woo patients to the hospital? What might work instead?
- How far will we go, vis-à-vis the competition, in merit-based aid to woo the brightest students to the college? What might work instead?
- Will we have a brighter future as a service agency if we merge, remain independent, or spin off a for-profit subsidiary?
- How do we build a new science center that reflects the special commitment of this coeducational college to prepare women scientists, a market niche we want to cultivate further?

that sharpen institutional priorities and ensure a strategic approach to the organization's future." In other words, effective boards both oversee strategic planning procedures (Type I) and work with management to determine what matters most to the long-term future of the organization (Type II).

The position we take here represents a shift in emphasis. We share the view expressed by Hamel and Prahalad (1997) that formal planning processes are too often "strategy as form filling.... turning the crank on the planning process once a year... [going] through the motions of an annual planning cycle... [producing] weighty strategic plans that adorn executive book cases," all without any "clue as to whether a company has a truly unique and stretching point of view about the future." In short, process becomes ritual, with the board largely on the sidelines. Strategic planning exercises rarely drill to the core questions of institutional identity, outmoded assumptions, and breakthrough strategies. Unless and until ideas, rather than plans, are the drive motors of strategy, the full range of trustees' talents will be vastly underutilized. As strategies are hatched and plans unfold, boards, along with CEOs, should be more akin to architects than general contractors or, worse, tradesmen. In order to fulfill this role boards must work in a strategic, not fiduciary, mode.

PROCESSES AND STRUCTURES FOR TYPE II GOVERNING

We previously termed the alignment of board activity with strategic priorities *The New Work of the Nonprofit Board* (Taylor, Chait, and Holland, 1996). The board was conceptualized as a strategic asset for the organization, not simply the overseer of the CEO's work. Strategic governance "harness[es] the collective efforts of accomplished [trustees] to advance the institution's mission and long-term welfare." Unlike the fiduciary mode, Type II governance aims to *construct,* not merely certify, a consensus about what the organization's strategy should be. To do this "new work," trustees and management need to work differently; the processes and structures proper for fiduciary governance will not do.

As in architecture, form should follow function. The board's committee structure, meetings, and channels of communication must be modified to foster strategic thinking and to cultivate a true strategic partnership with management. These are the essential purposes of Type II governance.

Partnerships are inevitably more complicated than crystal clear divisions of labor. Lines of authority, so important to Type I boards and CEOs, become blurred in Type II mode. Precisely due to the emphasis on strategic thinking, an activity not as easily compartmentalized as strategic planning, the realm and role of the board on one hand, and management on the other hand, cannot be entirely disentangled. Like partners in doubles tennis, neither party in Type II governance can afford to be particularly territorial or both will lose. This shift from board as monitor to board as partner spawns three major changes in practice.

1. *Board structure.* The nature of strategic work necessitates a flexible board structure. It is nearly impossible for a board to govern in Type II mode while wedded to an immutable Type I structure with functionally oriented committees. Administratively oriented committees are *destined* to delve into operations. Each has a separate and distinct sphere of responsibility; each necessarily oversees the work of one or more senior officers of

the organization. As so many stovepipes or silos, the committees generally select depth over breadth, and micromanagement over strategic governance. The structure constrains strategic thinking because, by definition, strategic issues cross functional boundaries. How does a university board, for instance, with committees on academic affairs, student life, admissions, finance, facilities, and development, address strategically vital questions like student retention, the climate for diversity, the impact of technology, competitive position, or tensions among multiple missions? Each problem transcends the purview of any one committee, and most cannot be resolved without attention to some portion of the portfolio of other committees.

To govern in Type II mode, the board's structure must be adapted to strategic priorities, not vice versa. Committees must mirror the organization's strategic imperatives, not the administration's organizational chart. The question changes from "What work does management have for this committee to do?" to "What is the most important work the board must organize to do?" Fiduciary committees, such as finance and investments, may remain to handle routine (and still important) matters as necessary. However, as a matter of both principle and practice, the board now organizes flexibly around strategic priorities, not rigidly around administrative operations. The board's structure should respond to matters of consequence to the organization, not to the convenient conventions of trustees and executives.

Trustees can use two devices to ensure that a new structure does not become as ossified as the old one. First, the board can rely more on task forces and ad hoc work groups where trustees, often with other constituencies, handle strategy-driven, time-specific, outcomes-oriented imperatives. When the work is done, the group disbands, an approach common to executive searches and capital campaigns yet, oddly enough, not replicated for equally appropriate tasks. (Exhibit 4.3 lists some assignments appropriate to multiconstituent task forces.) Second, the board's governance (or executive) committee can conduct a review process, perhaps every other year, to determine whether the trustees' committee structure matches organizational priorities. Should certain committees be merged or consolidated? Should any be eliminated? Should others meet on an as-needed basis only? What did this committee do over the past two years that was strategically indispensable? What work

---

EXHIBIT 4.3   BOARD TASK FORCE ASSIGNMENTS

- *Community image.* What specific steps can we take as a board and staff to improve the organization's image and reputation in the community?
- *Peer institutions.* Identify peer institutions we could use as a basis for comparison on multiple, strategic performance indicators.
- *Organizational benchmarks.* Identify a few organizations that excel in certain key areas of performance and learn the reasons that account for their success.
- *Staff development.* Examine the personal and professional development opportunities we currently offer staff. How effective are these programs? What else could we do?
- *Dashboards.* Develop two dashboards, each with no more than 12 indicators, one to monitor organizational performance, the other to monitor the board's performance.
- *Technology.* How might we use technology to make the board more effective, efficient, and knowledgeable?
- *Marketing.* Work with an external consultant to develop a marketing plan for the organization.
- *Board and trustee assessment.* Develop processes for regular assessment of individual trustees and the board as a whole.

might that committee do over the next two years to meet the same standard? Trustees keen to "sunset" obsolete organizational programs might profitably apply the same discipline to board committees.

In the fiduciary mode, trustees see the board's permanent committee structure as a sign of stability and an effective way to oversee management. In the strategic mode, trustees recognize that organizational strategies and priorities change, and that the board's committee structure must adapt accordingly. Otherwise, more often than not, trustees will not do much more than monitor whether the trains run on time to reach destinations decided by others—and both the board and management court the risk that new modes of competition will be ignored.

2. *Board and committee meetings.* The ritualized agendas and standardized formats of a Type I board meeting are ill-adapted to Type II work. There are too many *pro forma* reports and presentations and too few opportunities to set and tackle strategic priorities. Relatively trivial matters displace strategically significant issues. There is rarely even time for the CEO to think aloud with the board about incipient concerns or unexpected developments. Elsewhere (Chait, Holland, and Taylor, 1996), we recommended a host of techniques (for example, annual agendas, consent agendas, time guidelines, discussion questions, and "fireside chats" with the CEO) that make board meetings more meaningful and consequential.[1]

As with board structure, form should follow function. Most important, there should be occasions, some structured, others not, for trustees to think strategically—sometimes in response

---

[1]In Chapter 6, we provide still other devices to encourage robust discussion that are applicable here as well.

to management, sometimes in response to events, and sometimes simply at the request of the board. The question on the table is, "What's the big idea?" As James Barksdale, former CEO of Netscape, commented about how to lead a business in constant flux, "The main thing is to be damn sure that the main thing is really the main thing." In other words, boards should find and focus on the strategic bull's-eye while management lays plans to gather the bows and arrows and to shoot straight. (Exhibit 4.4 describes a simple exercise any board can use to see whether the trustees are thoughtfully and strategically engaged.)

3. *Communication and information.* The insularity of the Type I board and the attendant show-and-tell sessions will not support or advance Type II work. To think strategically, trustees must understand what influential internal and external stakeholders think as well. At this stage, trustees need only intelligent questions, not brilliant answers. The answers will emerge from two-way communication with a cross-section of constituents, as when conversations with stakeholders prompted a foundation to concentrate on intervention programs for at-risk preschool-

---

EXHIBIT 4.4   STRATEGIC THINKING

Invite a few peers, generally unfamiliar with the mission of your organization, to observe two consecutive board meetings. At the end of the second meeting, ask the outsiders to identify the most important strategic challenges to the organization that the board *thinks* about. If the answers contradict the trustees' impressions of what matters most (or worse, if the guests saw no evidence of strategic thinking), then surely the content and format of board meetings needs to be revamped. In Type II mode, trustees at board and committee meetings should, as much as possible, be thinking and talking about "the main thing."

ers, or when discussions with professional staff and community leaders persuaded the board and CEO of a museum to launch programs targeted at local arts teachers and inner-city school children.

Beyond constituents, direct access to experts can also strengthen a board's ability to uncover and then think strategically about complex, important questions. Some experts may already be on the board—the minister on a seminary board, the ecologist on an aquarium board, or the social worker on a hospice board. In other cases, the resources may be outside consultants. On a Type I board, these experts would advise only the CEO or the senior staff. The board might not know what the consultants recommended and why, or which features of the consultant's report were accepted and what elements were rejected. Access to unfiltered information and unfettered opportunities to ask questions of experts precipitate greater insight and better questions.

In addition to comparative perspectives, Type II governance requires comparative data, especially information that can be analyzed across institutions and over time. In the fiduciary mode, boards need data to ensure organizational compliance. Type I boards are prone to request all the data all the time as a way to make management accountable and as a means to check for problems. In the strategic mode, boards also use data to understand organizational performance relative to plans and peers. Objective, trend-line data, clearly linked to strategic priorities, permit a board to assess progress, spot downturns and, ultimately, rethink strategy. Devices like "dashboards" (Chait, Holland, and Taylor, 1996), "balanced scorecards" (Kaplan and Norton, 1996), or "strategic indicators" (Taylor and Massy, 1996) equip boards to track data on institutional performance, capacity, and condition. The information spotlights not only areas ripe for tactical adjustments, but areas where conventional

EXHIBIT 4.5	COMPARING TYPE I AND TYPE II GOVERNANCE

Type I Governance	Type II Governance
Management defines problems and opportunities; develops formal plans. Board listens and learns; approves and monitors.	Board and management think together to discover strategic priorities and drivers.
Board structure parallels administrative functions. Premium on permanency.	Board structure mirrors organization's strategic priorities. Premium on flexibility.
Board meetings process driven. Function follows form. Protocol rarely varies.	Board meetings content-driven. Form follows function. Protocol often varies.
Staff transmits to board large quantities of technical data from few sources.	Board and staff discuss strategic data from multiple sources.

strategy needs to be reexamined and new ideas entertained. The questions before the board subtly change from "How do we maintain market share?" to "Are we in the right markets?" or from "How much debt capacity do we have?" to "Where do we want to invest (or disinvest)?"

Exhibit 4.5 summarizes the key differences between the structures and processes of Type I and Type II governance.

IMPLEMENTING STRATEGY

Faithful to the precept that trustees set policies that management administers, Type I boards eschew almost any role in executing strategy—with the notable exceptions of fund-raising and external advocacy, which *are* implementation. In these cases, even the most ardent advocates among CEOs for separation of power readily waive the rules. In all other situations, however, Type I boards live by the old adage "Noses in, fingers out."

In Type II mode, boards play a more active role, particularly as technical assistants. For instance, board members may be integrally involved in efforts to execute a contract with a new strategic partner, to upgrade technology, or to acquire property or facilities necessary to expand consistent with the organization's strategic plan. We previously proposed three circumstances when board engagement in strategy implementation might be warranted: (1) the chair *and* CEO believe that one or more trustees could best handle a task; (2) participation in implementation would be instructive for trustees; and (3) involvement would inform trustees about whether the organization was on course and on mission (Chait and Taylor, 1989).

In retrospect, these guidelines for boards now seem more appropriate for organizations engaged in formal planning cycles. The criteria, while still useful under those circumstances, position the board as fiduciary monitors and technical experts. Trustees are otherwise off the hook (and out of the loop). There is no recognition that the board could, for example, be a fruitful source of tactics, trade-offs, performance metrics, midcourse corrections, and organizational discipline, all valuable contributions to strategy execution. These omissions severely constrict the board's role and value in strategy implementation. Exhibit 4.6 describes an exercise to pinpoint the crucial contributions the board must make (or has made) in order to translate plans and ideas into actions and achievements without undue concern for the canonical strictures of governance.

WHY NOT JUST TYPES I AND II?

We have made the case for the centrality of both fiduciary and strategic governance. Both are vital. Nearly every board today

EXHIBIT 4.6	THE BOARD'S PART IN ACHIEVING STRATEGIC GOALS

This exercise directs attention to the board's *indispensable* contributions to the realization of strategic priorities. For each priority, the board, along with the CEO, should define success—what constitutes a successful outcome. Then, individually or in small work groups, trustees should "fast forward" to a future time when the intended results have presumably been achieved. With that picture in mind, board members should complete the following sentence:

"This priority would not have been achieved if the board had not _____."

For instance:
- The quality and quantity of applicants to the college would not have increased had the board not _____.
- The orchestra's financial condition would not have stabilized if the board had not _____.
- The museum would not have become a "destination" for a cross-section of the community had the board not _____.
- The hospital would not have survived the challenges of managed care unless the board _____.
- The treatment center would not have become a career placement center as well if the board had not _____.
- Revenues from earned income at the association would not have nearly doubled unless the board _____.

The responses to these questions should be shared anonymously with the entire board and senior management as a way to pinpoint the trustees' essential roles in execution of the strategic plan. *The same process can be used retrospectively. The questions can be altered to ask what the board did (or did not) do that best explains the attainment (or failure) of previous strategic priorities.*

practices some form of fiduciary governance; most participate (to varying degrees) in the development, approval, and oversight of strategic plans. Many even provide technical assistance to enact the plan. In the terminology of technology, formal planning is like an older version of software. Call it TII.1. It still works, but newer versions do more and perform better. Strategic governance, or TII.2, encourages trustees to think about issues that really matter and strategies that might really work. Professional staff and technicians then convert these ideas into a plan, nested in a competitive context and intended to enhance the organization's value to its constituents.

This may sound like quite enough to many trustees and executives. The best of Types I and II governance, taken together, do indeed comprise the current state of the art in trusteeship. But there is a missing piece that becomes evident when we view nonprofit organizations in a different light that reveals a world less orderly and more complex than most board members and nonprofit executives acknowledge. In this environment:

- Nonprofits are more than rational strategies and logical plans.
- Organizations are also cultures, political systems, and symbolic contexts.
- The sense people make of events often matters more than the events themselves.
- Much of what drives strategy occurs before strategic planning starts, and before boards engage the process.
- Strategies sometimes emerge despite plans or apart from plans.

These attributes necessitate a third, largely unrecognized, yet equally critical mode of trusteeship: generative governance.

CHAPTER 5

Type III: Generative Thinking

In moving from fiduciary and strategic governance to generative governance, we enter territory that is at once familiar to trustees yet new to nonprofit boards. In their "day jobs" as managers, professionals, or leaders of organizations, trustees routinely rely on generative thinking, so much so that they have no need to name it or analyze it. They just do it. But in the boardroom, trustees are at a double disadvantage. Most boards do not routinely practice generative thinking. And because they do not have the necessary language and frameworks to discuss it, trustees often overlook three propositions central to Type III governing: (1) how powerful generative thinking is; (2) how vital it is to governing; and (3) how nearly everyone in a nonprofit, *except* the board, uses it to influence the organization. In other words, boards are often not present when and where the most important action occurs. When it comes to generative governing, most trustees add too little, too late.

This chapter and the next one address how to change that. In this chapter, we describe the generative thinking that underlies generative governance. In the next chapter, we discuss how boards can put these ideas into practice.

Generative thinking provides a sense of problems and opportunities. When individuals produce a new sense of things through generative thinking, others admire their "wisdom," "insight," or "creativity." When an entire field or profession gains a new perspective, we recognize it as a "paradigm shift." After the shift, nothing looks the same. For example, many of the injuries children suffered at the hands of their parents were once considered the result of accidents. Now these "accidents" are recognized as child abuse (Weick, 1995). Similarly, the broken windows of derelict buildings were typically seen as the mark of a crime-ridden neighborhood, but are now considered a *cause* of crime as well. This sense inspired a new strategy of community policing, where the job of police is to help neighborhoods *prevent* broken windows as part of a larger effort to create order and safety (Kelling and Coles, 1996).

Somewhere between the insights of individuals and the paradigm shifts of fields lies the equally important, but less recognized, generative thinking of organizations. As organizational theorist Jeffrey Pfeffer has noted, establishing "the framework within which issues will be viewed and decided is often tantamount to determining the result" (1992). If this is true, then little, if anything, can be more important to organizations, or to a conception of governance, than generative thinking.

THE POWER OF GENERATIVE THINKING IN ORGANIZATIONS

Typically, we locate much of the power and opportunity to shape an institution in familiar organizational processes like mission setting, strategy development, and problem solving. Because they produce the purposes, strategies, and ideas that drive organizations, these are recognized as powerful processes. But a fourth process, of generative thinking, is actually more powerful. Generative thinking precedes these. More to the point, it *generates* the other processes.

To return to the paradigm shifts, imagine that a single non-profit, rather than a loose network of police officers, researchers, and policy makers, first developed the strategy of community policing. It would be natural to credit the organization's strategy-development process for the new approach to fighting crime. But how could this really be? The organization would need the *idea*, if not the label, of community policing in order to arrive at the strategy and associated tactics. Strategy development helps an organization get from here to there, from the present point A to a future, preferred point B. But understanding point A— in this case, to conclude that the deployment of police was no longer a sufficient response to crime—must come first. And generative thinking produces a vision of point B—in this case, the idea of a different, preventive approach. Without generative thinking, we would have neither here nor there.

In fact, most of the formal planning and learning processes that appear so powerful in organizations look incomplete when one takes generative thinking into account. For example, businesses routinely invested in formal product-development processes to get an idea from the drawing board to the marketplace. The product development process was a series of engineering, manufacturing, and marketing activities. But then some product developers wondered if there was not more to the process. After all, how did ideas reach the drawing board in the first place? And what would increase the chances of developing good ideas to start with (Deschamps and Nayak, 1995)? In effect, the key question was, "What kind of generative thinking precedes product development?"

The same is true of organizational problem solving. Whether conducted through formal program development or informal trial-and-error, the important work of "problem framing" (Schon, 1983) precedes problem solving. Before we solve a problem, we decide upon the nature of the problem. Similarly, the scientific method has value only *after* we find a hypothesis worth testing (Polanyi, 1974). Invariably, great research starts with great questions.

However compelling that logic may be, it has little influence on the way organizations usually work. In fact, judging from the amount of attention most of us give generative thinking, it is as if we believe that goals, missions, and problems simply appear in organizations, much as seventeenth-century Europeans believed that a jar full of old rags and wheat husks, left open for a few weeks, would spontaneously generate flies. It took nearly a century for people to speculate that flies might be depositing eggs into the jars. From there, a different understanding soon became obvious: An unseen biological process, not piles of rags and wheat husks, was generating new life. The same is true of organizations. A prior, unexamined cognitive process generates the moral commitments that missions codify, the goals that strategies advance, and the diagnoses that problem solving addresses.

INSIDE THE BLACK BOX
OF GENERATIVE THINKING

The process of generative thinking is a classic "black box" phenomenon: We can see and appreciate what it produces but we have little sense of how the work actually gets done. In some cases, there seems to be little point in trying to understand it. For instance, it is clear that some individuals have a gift for generative thinking, but that others cannot acquire it by studying some step-by-step process. Similarly, we can appreciate that powerful paradigm shifts transform entire fields, industries, or societies, but that no one person can control the process. Organizations are different. We *do* attempt to govern and control organizations. To the degree we can understand the process of generative thinking, we might be able to encourage, support, and leverage it, much as we do other, arguably less important, organizational processes. It is worth lifting the lid to see what is inside the box.

It turns out, however, that opening the black box is easier than describing what goes on inside. One sees a welter of subtle, counterintuitive, or vaguely familiar phenomena that are not normally dissected and discussed. But the theorists' description of this work can offer practitioners a great deal,[1] not because it reveals something entirely new, but because it makes clear analytically what many understand intuitively. It is at that point that new possibilities for governing emerge.

The generative process is easiest to grasp by starting at the end, describing the results of generative thinking, and then looking backwards to see what produces that output. As Karl Weick has argued, before an organization develops strategies or solves problems, it generates another cognitive product: sense or meaning (Weick, 1995). The sense that generative thinking

---

[1]We use the term "generative thinking" to refer to a cognitive process that dozens of theorists in several disciplines have, in whole or part, described by different names. Among those whose ideas have helped us reconsider governance are: Karl Weick ("sense-making"); Donald Schon ("reflective practice"); Henry Mintzberg ("emergent strategy"); Ronald Heifetz ("adaptive leadership"); Michael Polanyi ("personal knowledge"); Robert Birnbaum ("cognitive complexity"); Lee Bolman and Terrence Deal ("framing organizations"); and James March and Michael Cohen ("sensible foolishness").

produces is not the same as knowledge, information, or data. Rather, generative thinking produces a sense of what knowledge, information, and data *mean*. The generative thinking that preceded community policing made sense of information already in hand by reframing the problem that the information depicted. Data on rising crime did not dictate either conventional crime-fighting *or* community policing; people making sense of the data did that.

The process of problem-framing or sense-making is subjective. The same information could have inspired different conceptions of the problem. In fact, even as community policing grew popular, one police commissioner redefined the problem by arguing that his police department lacked the information needed to spot incipient crime waves and the data needed to hold officers accountable for their performance. He framed the problem as a managerial one. The result was a new management process driven by information technology (Dewan, 2004). Proponents of community policing and police management used the same data but made different sense of it. And the sense they produced led to different strategies. It is precisely because sense-making is so subjective and involves so many choices that it is so powerful and, ultimately, so necessary to governing.

The paradigm shifts show sense-making at an epic, high-stakes scale. But sense-making shapes organizations in more prosaic, though still important, ways. Everyone can recall moments when their sense of things at work changed profoundly. They remark: "When you put it that way, it does make sense" or "When I look at it that way, I do see things in a different light." What they tend to overlook is *how* things get put a different way, a process that involves three steps:

1. Noticing cues and clues.   How do people get from the same data to different, even conflicting, senses of what the data mean? In part, they notice and focus on different cues (Weick, 1995). They construct a meaningful proposition by seeing or emphasizing only some of the countless stimuli competing for their attention. When police analysts look at crime data, but also notice and think about the prevalence of broken windows, they might begin to wonder how a community can either be hostile or hospitable to criminal activity. This could put them on a path toward community policing. When they look at crime data, but also notice the dearth of statistical reports available to police officers, they might begin to wonder about the state of police management. This could put them on a path toward new supervisory practices. The cues and clues people heed shape the problems they see and the strategies they develop. And because environments are made up of innumerable events, facts, people, and phenomena, the people whose cues gain an organization's attention exercise enormous power.

But how do people select cues? What increases the chances of choosing cues that will lead organizations to better goals, better questions, and a better sense of problems and opportunities?

2. Choosing and using frames.   We all rely on sense-making to cope with environments that otherwise would not make sense. Ranganath Nayak, a student of organizational innovation, describes the period before people arrive at a promising product idea as the "fuzzy front end" of the product-development process. People do not know where to look, what to notice, or how to start the search for new ideas (Letts, Ryan, and Grossman, 1999). Precisely because there is so much to see, little or nothing is in focus. Schon described as "problematic situations" or, more succinctly, a "mess" the period when the professional recognizes that something is wrong, but does not yet understand the problem (1983).

People use frames to help make sense of their environments. Sometimes they use frames unconsciously or reflexively, as when they look at things through the familiar prism of their profession. (Lawyers hardly notice they are using a legal frame.) Frames can also be values-based. People with a commitment to equity will tend to look at how decisions might marginalize some and favor others. Temperaments are frames of sorts, which determine whether we see situations as problems or opportunities. The frames help us understand, and understanding helps us act. Because frames cause people to notice some cues and not others, or reorganize information into meaningful patterns, they are critical determinants of sense-making. As Weick has insightfully stated, "Believing is seeing" (1995). People notice what they are predisposed to see based on the frames they use.

This is not to say that people are prisoners of their frames. We can consciously look at a situation through different frames to generate new sense-making options. The capacity to use multiple frames is central to recent leadership theory. "Cognitively complex" leaders (Birnbaum, 1992) use more frames more often and, therefore, see more problems and opportunities in more ways. In *Reframing Organizations*, Lee Bolman and Terrence Deal (1997) describe four frames that leaders can use to perceive and understand organizational situations (see Exhibit 5.1). For instance, looking through a "structural frame," managers may see the problem of staff turnover as a matter of compensation and incentive systems, whereas a human resource frame may suggest

EXHIBIT 5.1   FOUR FRAMES

Structural Frame. Focus on authority, rules, regulations, priorities, policies, procedures, plans, chain of command, and performance control.

Human Resource Frame. Focus on relationship or "fit" between people and organization, members' needs, skills, fulfillment, commitment, and professional development.

Political Frame. Focus on exercise of power, constituents, coalitions, conflict, compromise, bargaining, negotiating, and allocation of resources.

Symbolic Frame. Focus on organizational culture, meaning, beliefs, stories, rituals, ceremonies, myths, spirit, and expression.

Adapted from *Reframing Organizations: Artistry, Choice, and Leadership* (Bolman and Deal, 1997)

that quality of work life or lack of professional autonomy could be the problem. Using a political frame, trustees might regard a controversy over a college mascot as a power struggle among constituencies, while a symbolic frame would highlight the signal transmitted about diversity. In short, frames rule.

3. Thinking retrospectively.   We are all conditioned not to "dwell on the past" or let the organization get "stuck in the past." We tend to believe leaders should be "out ahead," drawing people into the future through "forward thinking." But people actually make sense by thinking about the past, not the future. By the time they are framed, the cues and clues we rely on for sense-making are in the past.

This insight threatens nearly all the assumptions and practices of formal strategy development. Sense-making advocates like Weick discount future-oriented strategy work—the "forecasting, contingency planning, strategic planning, and other magical probes into the future"—as "wasteful and misleading" (Weick, 1995). As we discussed in Chapter 4, Henry Mintzberg has argued that not all strategy comes from formal planning processes that extrapolate from the present to the future and then detail plans to get there (1994). In contrast to "deliberate" or "intended" strategy, Mintzberg maintains that strategy often just emerges out of the organization's ongoing work (1994). People look back over the organization's past and, through sense-making, uncover new patterns already in place, even if previously unnoticed, that suggest new strategies. Emergent strategy entails discovery; deliberate strategy entails design.

This does not mean that strategy operates by laws of karma, where past events ordain future choices. We still have the power to decide the meaning of past events. We can make sense of the past in many ways, and each might suggest a different future. Power rests with people armed with the knowledge and eloquence to craft an organization's "dominant narrative" or operative version of "history." Rosabeth Kanter, a noted authority on leadership, stressed that the power to construct (or reconstruct) the past begets the power to shape the future.

> In conceiving of a different future, [innovators] have to be historians as well. When innovators begin to define a project..., they are not only seeing what is possible, they may be learning more about the past; and one of the prime uses of the past is in the construction of a story that makes the future seem to grow naturally out of it in terms compatible with the organization's culture (1983).

Constructing a dominant narrative involves much more than insisting on a version of the past through propaganda or "spin."

A successful narrative works because it is compelling, not because it is coercive. It offers a coherent story that appeals to people's sensibilities, values, and traditions.

■ ■ ■

This account of generative thinking provides both a new frame for viewing organizations and a new vocabulary for discussing what we see. When we look at nonprofit organizations through this frame, we now notice something very important: *Generative thinking is essential to governing.* As long as governing means what most people think it means—setting the goals and direction of an organization and holding management accountable for progress toward those goals—then generative thinking has to be essential to governing. Generative thinking is where goal-setting and direction-setting originate. The contributions boards make to mission-setting, strategy-development, and problem solving certainly shape organizations. But it is *cues* and *frames*, along with *retrospective thinking*, that enable the *sense-making* on which these other processes depend. And a closer examination of nonprofits suggests something else: Although generative work is essential to governing, boards do very little of it.

TOWARD GENERATIVE GOVERNING

When viewed through the lens of generative thinking, we can see four different governance scenarios (see Exhibit 5.2 on page 98). Two are especially dysfunctional, a third is prevalent but problematic, and a fourth is uncommon yet much preferred. One variable defines the scenarios: the degree of relative engagement by trustees and executives in generative work. We start with the most common scenario.

Leadership as Governance: Executives Displace Trustees

To understand the potential of generative governance, we must first understand what most organizations have now. In most nonprofits, CEOs, aided by senior staff, are presumed to be the organization's most influential generative thinkers. Once we recognize generative thinking as a cognitive process that belongs to governance, we see that many nonprofits really rely on their leaders to *govern*. In fact, as we look more closely, we realize that most CEOs use methods of deliberation and consultation that constitute a virtual governing process. When executives displace trustees, we have, in effect, leadership as governance.

Leaders as Generative Thinkers.   The theory and practice of leadership in recent years has been transformed by one proposition. As Max DuPree declared, "The first responsibility of the leader is to define reality" (DuPree as cited in Gergen and Kellerman, 2000). Or as L. Thayer states: "A leader is one who alters or guides the manner in which his followers 'mind' the world. The leader is a sense-giver" (Thayer, as quoted in Weick, 1995). Heifetz's distinction between "technical" and "adaptive" problems makes the same point (1994). Although effective organizational leaders are rarely described in these terms, the hallmarks of their work are clear. Leaders frame problems with memorable language (for example, "I have a dream"); use vivid, sense-giving images (for example, battered children); and use meaningful metaphors (for example, the War on Poverty). All of these actions shape what people perceive and generate a course of action.

It is hardly surprising that leadership entails something as powerful as generative thinking. From there, it is easy to mistakenly conclude that gifted leaders carry the burden of sense-making alone, as suggested by the images of leader as sense-*giver* or reality-*definer*. But the leader should be one sense-maker among many, all engaged in a collective process of generative thinking that the leader may facilitate.

Leadership as a Governing Process. Good leaders do not just contribute generative insights to their organizations; they also engage others in generative thinking. Many have a formally designated "leadership team" that works with them to set agendas, identify priorities, develop plans, and engage in generative thinking as well. In professional nonprofits, doctors, social workers, curators, or faculty also help the organization, formally and informally, to grapple with ambiguous situations, frame new problems, and make sense of events. Some trustees occasionally participate, too, although usually as members of the CEO's "kitchen cabinet." And especially when organizations require consensus on a newly framed problem, a nonprofit's constituents—whether students, patients, or clients—also participate. Executives also rely on actors outside the organization, including funders, consultants, and colleagues as sources of generative thinking. In other words, in many nonprofits, no one has a monopoly on generative thinking.

Because the adaptive problems that leaders help their organizations frame involve "changes in values, belief, and behavior"

(Heifetz, 1994), they almost inevitably provoke disagreements. Unlike technical innovations, generative constructs like community policing and battered children force people to confront fundamental beliefs and behaviors. Part of a leader's responsibility is to facilitate consensus on such contested issues. By consulting and engaging an organization's many stakeholders, leaders generate not just a sense of the situation, but also a commitment, or "buy-in," to take actions consistent with that consensus. In Heifetz's formulation, "Leaders mobilize people to face problems, and communities make progress on problems because leaders challenge and help them to do so" (1994). A consensus about adaptive problems will govern the organization's strategic and technical work. Leaders who facilitate that consensus are, in effect, governing their organizations.

This new leadership theory repositions technical managers as "adaptive" or "cognitively complex" leaders engaged in the generative thinking essential to governing. This raises an urgent question: Where do boards fit into the picture?

Boards as Bystanders. Most boards are on the outside looking in, as virtually everyone else in and around the organization participates in generative work. True, some boards do generative work some of the time, and a few trustees regularly do so, but most boards are not organized and equipped to do generative work. As we argued earlier, boards have increasingly practiced a managerial version of governance. Instead of identifying problems, framing issues, or making sense of the organization, most boards address the problems that managers present to them. Indeed, the "no-board scenario"[2] suggests that

---

[2]For more on no-board scenario, see p. 18.

boards often do not even *contribute* to, let alone lead, their organization's generative work. When trustees and executives describe what would happen if their board "hibernated" for several years, no one worries that the organization would be deprived of powerful ideas, keen insights, or important perspectives on problems.

Even when vigorous debate does occur, board discussion invariably remains embedded within the initial frame constructed by management. From time to time, a trustee will recommend that the board think "outside the box," basically a plea to reframe the issue. Usually, the suggestion goes unheeded as a fanciful proposal from an unrealistic or disruptive trustee. Most boards proceed to slightly modify and then ratify management's solutions to management's versions of the organization's problems. An occasion to govern the organization thus becomes merely a chance to counsel management. In the process, the entity granted ultimate power exercises precious little influence.

Governance by Default: Trustees and Executives Disengage

When neither executives nor trustees think generatively, governance by default results. Staff fill the vacuum with various versions of organizational reality, with different, possibly dissonant implications for mission, strategies, and programs. Instead of a shared sense of meaning, organizations face a shifting, contested, and unarticulated web of meanings. Some theorists describe these conditions as "organized anarchy" (Cohen and March, 1974), where leaders, and certainly trustees, are just one voice among many in a fluid, if not chaotic environment. Such organizations are influenced more than governed.

External actors also impose their own sense and meaning on the organization. Funders do more than just give money, professional networks supply more than information, and consultants add more than expertise. They all influence the organization by contributing meaning to it. To prevent the organization from being defined entirely by others, leaders of the organization and leaders of the board need to orchestrate generative thinking, not to suppress the contributions of others but to nurture and, as much as possible, harmonize the many voices needed to create a chorus of consensus.

Governance by Fiat: Trustees Displace Executives

If generative thinking is central to governing and boards are bystanders, then one response might be to assign all generative work to boards. But if trustees do all the generative work, then governance by fiat would result, barely an improvement over governance by default. Boards would impose their views on executives, an arrangement few executives and trustees would tolerate. Most boards recognize that staff, particularly the CEO, are not only entitled to a pivotal role in generative work, but well-positioned to do the work. Arguably, more than anyone else, CEOs have access to the innumerable cues, clues, and constituents that inspire sense-making. They also understand the values of the organization that inform sense-making. Even boards eager to participate in generative governance would be reluctant to exclude executives.

Type III Governance: Trustees and Executives Collaborate

If we resist the temptation to treat generative work as a zero-sum contest for power, we can see another possibility where trustees and executives work together, connecting the organization's formal governing processes with the powerful but largely informal work of generative thinking.

Because we resolutely regard this as shared work, we cannot offer what the board-improvement field so often promises trustees and executives: a set of bright lines that neatly divide the board's work (policy, strategy, and governance) from the staff's (administration, implementation, and management). It simply makes no sense to reserve generative work for boards when leaders are vital to the process, or to reserve for leaders work that belongs at the heart of governance. Generative work demands a fusion of thinking, not a division of labor.[3]

The vast majority of boards are likely to do the vast majority of Type III work in tandem with executives. This work can take two forms.

Overseeing generative work. Trustees can oversee generative work, much as they do the strategy recommendations executives present to them when they do Type II governing. Rather than create strategy, trustees question assumptions, probe feasibility, identify obstacles and opportunities, all to improve the chances for success. Similarly, boards can review and critique the gener-

---

[3]There are some occasions when a board might want to deliberate in a generative mode without an executive present. For example, trustees use leadership transitions as a time to take stock of the organization's challenges, aspirations, and values, all of which clarify the qualities and experience that trustees want in the next CEO. Trustees may also operate this way when CEOs are embroiled in controversy. Beyond considering the embattled executive's views, the board deliberates alone to arrive at its own sense of the problem. Finally, boards might occasionally meet apart from CEOs to ask, in effect, "Has the CEO been framing matters in a meaningful way?"

ative thinking of executives: probing how they arrived at their sense of a problem or opportunity, identifying alternative ways of framing the issue, and exploring the sense of the past embedded in their proposals for the future. The point is not for trustees to displace or control staff, but to offer executives a venue to test those views with a supportive, inquisitive board.

This is, in effect, what executives do with trustees who serve as "sounding boards." They turn to trustees, individually or as a group, for advice on "sticky" situations: an ambiguous personnel problem, a potential conflict with a donor, or an emerging conflict with public policy. The executives share their generative thinking-in-process to get guidance and assistance from trustees *before* the matter reaches the board for formal consideration or action.

Through these exchanges, trustees also hold executives accountable. Boards that oversee executives in Types I and II track the flow of tangible assets and monitor progress toward strategic goals. In Type III oversight, trustees gauge the generative thinking of executives, subjecting this powerful work to the same scrutiny boards are now expected to give to financial and strategic work.

Initiating generative work. Trustees and executives can work in tandem to initiate generative work, in the same way that some boards and executives work together to develop strategies. Although it is sometimes useful for an executive or a board member to propose a sense of a situation as a point of departure, a deliberative group can also initiate the work. For most boards, this entails a new type of agenda that features ambiguous or problematic situations rather than reports and routine motions. Instead of winning the board's confidence by masking all ambiguities, an executive can earn the board's trust by exposing the ambiguities and then grappling together to make sense of the situation.

This is where trustees and executives make good on the lip service so often paid to "brainstorming," "thinking out of the box," and "diversity of perspectives." We detail the practices that support this work in the next chapter; suffice it to say here that this is where powerful generative work can become powerful governing work, precisely because trustees and executives do the work jointly. Like copilots of commercial aircraft who typically take turns flying (alternating flight segments or, on longer journeys, after specified periods of time), trustees and executives can take turns initiating generative deliberations; one can lead and the other can respond. The captain (here, the board) reserves the final authority but rarely acts unilaterally, usually only when required by an emergency.

There is always the possibility that either executives or trustees will do generative work with little or no involvement of the other party. But these are not entirely equivalent "sins." There is a subtle difference with profound governing implications. When executives preemptively decide how (and how much) trustees will participate in generative work—work that is part and parcel of governing—they are, in effect, hijacking generative governance, and telling boards when and how they can govern. It is as if executives arrogate from boards the authority to govern in the generative mode, then delegate it back, as they deem appropriate. When boards preemptively exclude executives from a major role in generative work, they are probably making an unwise choice, but at least it is a choice they are authorized to make.

EXHIBIT 5.2 **GENERATIVE THINKING: FOUR SCENARIOS**

EXECUTIVE ENGAGEMENT

high

I *Governance by Fiat* Trustees Displace Executives	II *Type III Governance* Trustees and Executives Collaborate
III *Governance by Default* Trustees and Executives Disengage	IV *Leadership as Governance* Executives Displace Trustees

TRUSTEE ENGAGEMENT

low

When the engagement of both trustees and executives in generative work is high (Quadrant II), the result is optimal: Type III Governance. The other quadrants depict unbalanced engagements that lead to problematic situations. In Quadrant I, trustees commandeer most of the generative work, and impose the results on executives. This might be described as governance by fiat. In Quadrant III, neither executives nor trustees attend to generative work. This produces generative governance by default, where the generative work of other actors inside and outside the organization (for example, staff, funders, regulators, and industry groups) exert greater influence than trustees and executives over strategy, mission, and problem solving. In Quadrant IV, executives dominate generative work, which renders leadership as governance. (Problems of purpose, described in Chapter 2, are likely to be most acute here.)

■ ■ ■

Unlike much of the conventional guidance offered to boards, this image of shared generative governance does little to relieve anxieties about the ambiguity and uncertainty of board–staff relationships. But the board-improvement approaches that do promise precision, with specific and fixed roles for trustees and staff, usually involve a huge and generally unfavorable trade-off: more clarity but less governance, comfort at the cost of impact. Such neat divisions of labor succeed by *relieving* boards and staff of the challenge of working together on important issues. Few partnerships, none less than trustees and their chief executive, succeed on the strength of clear boundaries. When trustees and staff share the labor, the complexity of board-staff interactions is not eliminated. But the results do make the tensions worth bearing.

One question remains: Can boards do this work?

CAN BOARDS DO IT?

As it turns out, nonprofit boards are ideally positioned for generative governing work for three fundamental reasons: power, plurality, and position.

1. *Power.* Generative thinking is powerful; it shapes much of what happens in an organization. As a center of authority and legitimacy, boards have the power—indeed, the obligation—to perform generative work. In fact, the more power a process implies, the more boards should be expected to play a role.

2. *Plurality.* Generative work thrives on deliberations among participants with different perspectives and different frames

for noticing different cues and clues. The more hypotheses and angles of vision, the more likely perceptive reformulations and keen insights will materialize. Whereas an organization might hope that great minds will think more or less alike on fiduciary matters, generative work benefits from the interplay of ideas. Boards of trustees enrich the mix.

3. *Position.* Trustees are typically situated at the edge of the organization, close enough to understand the institution's aims, operations, and culture yet far enough removed to have some perspective, distance, and detachment. Board members usually embrace the institution's mission but have little at risk personally or professionally. From this vantage point, trustees can see the larger picture, overall patterns, and telltale anomalies reasonably well. Much as Heifetz encourages executives to lead from the "balcony" (1994), the board too enjoys an advantageous perch for sense-making.

In short, boards are right for generative work. Now we turn to doing this work right.

CHAPTER 6

Type III: Generative Governing

To convert the concepts of the previous chapter into effective boardroom practices, trustees can start with the First Law of Generative Governance: *The opportunity to influence generative work declines over time.* As Exhibit 6.1 illustrates, opportunity peaks when the organization faces a problematic or ambiguous situation, often no more than an ill-defined hunch that trouble or possibility looms. Precisely because nothing has been ruled out (or in), the opportunity to make sense of the situation will never be greater. This opportunity is high on the generative curve, where people rely on cues and clues, a sense of the past, and framing to generate new meaning and insights. Armed with new meaning, they then move down the curve to problem solving and strategy development. Obviously, work lower on the curve is important. What good is a cleverly framed problem without a solution, an attractive mission without a strategy, or a great plan without execution? Indeed, as proponents of a three-mode approach to governing, we do not advise that trustees spend all their time high on the curve. But if they want to engage in *generative* governing, trustees need to work there some of the time.

EXHIBIT 6.1   THE GENERATIVE CURVE*

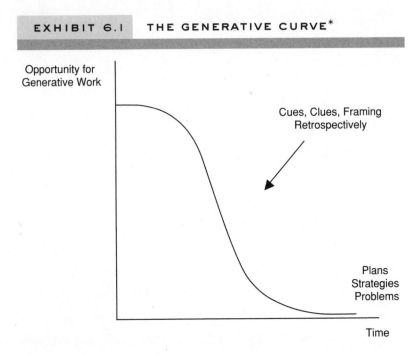

The opportunity for influence in generative work declines as issues are framed and converted into strategic options and plans over time.

---

* The curve is a modification of Deschamps and Nayak's product development curve (Letts et al., 1999).

Unfortunately, the curve will prove slippery for many boards. In fact, the First Law of Generative Governance suggests a companion hypothesis about boards and generative work: *Trustee involvement is lowest where generative opportunity is greatest, and trustee involvement increases as generative opportunity declines* (see Exhibit 6.2). In the very worst cases, trustees' involvement curve peaks after all the problems have been framed and the strategy developed. At that point, boards simply react to proposed strategies and oversee implementation of plans. They may be more diligent than the notorious rubber-stamp board, but these trustees

EXHIBIT 6.2   BOARDS AND GENERATIVE OPPORTUNITY

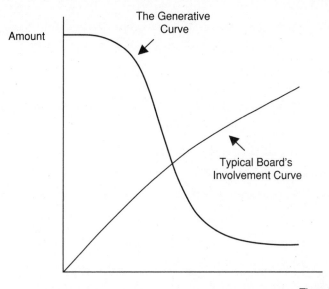

Hypothesis on Boards and Generative Work: Trustee involvement is lowest where generative opportunity is greatest, and trustee involvement increases as generative opportunity declines.

are still generative flatliners; they get involved only as the generative curve evens out.

Many boards stay low on the curve in part because they are comfortable there. They feel confident doing strategy and oversight, work they understand. Aided by familiar Type I and II mental maps, they can easily navigate the logical, productive organizational territory lower on the curve. And when plans, strategies, and proposals arrive in spiral-bound reports and Power-Point presentations, trustees have something to "sink their teeth into." Higher on the curve, where challenges have not been precisely framed, trustees are unsure where to look, what to discuss, and how to start. They lack the practices and tools needed for Type III work.

This chapter attempts to fill that gap by describing six resources, based on the concepts of Chapter 5, for working high on the generative curve:

1. A Type III mental map that describes the organizational terrain boards will find there
2. A review of the landmarks that signal generative opportunities may be at hand
3. Advice for working at the organizational boundaries, where conditions are conducive to generative thinking
4. Techniques for thinking about the past in order to move toward the future
5. Methods for promoting generative deliberation
6. Considerations for assessing the board's generative work

These resources are a starting point. Although we have seen generative thinking in action and generative moments in the board room, we have found no model or "best practice" of institutionalized generative governance to share. In this sense, these are resources for inventing, more than implementing, generative governance.

USING A TYPE III MENTAL MAP
OF THE ORGANIZATION

Type I and II mental maps depict the orderly grid of logic, plans, and strategies that trustees navigate lower on the generative curve. Higher on the curve, boards enter territory that is, by comparison, a wilderness. To navigate here, trustees need a mental map that depicts at least three features of the nonrational, generative organization.[1]

Goals are often ambiguous, if not contested. In Type I and II territory, a crisply articulated mission inspires a coherent strategy which, in turn, guides operations. In Type III territory, the goals at the top of the organization are at best provisional. Organizational purposes are not only multiple, complex, and abstract, but also fluid. Purposes that are paramount one year may be less so the next, and one constituency's top priority may be a matter of indifference to another. In other words, goals cannot be accepted as constants that organize everything else. Instead, the goals themselves have to be continuously reexamined and revised, and stakeholder commitment to them has to be secured again and again.

The future is uncertain. If leaders truly believed the future was entirely unpredictable, organizations could not function. Who could act in the face of utter uncertainty? But in Type III territory, it is just as misguided to assume that consistently useful predictions about the future are possible. Small, isolated, and some-

---

[1]The nonrational organization has been described as "organized anarchy" (Cohen and March, 1974) and "open system" (Scott, 2003) that can be understood in light of "complexity science" (Stacey, 1996). Beyond organizations, similar concepts have been applied, under the rubric of "chaos theory," (Scott, 2003) to the environment, and under the banner of "behavioral economics," (Dubner, 2003) to investing. These theories have one crucial common thread: organizations (and individuals) are not inherently and unfailingly rational, logical, or linear and, therefore, neither leaders nor strategies can be deterministic.

times random perturbations can produce widespread effects, especially when organizations (or industries or nations) are highly interdependent or "tightly coupled" (Weick, 1976). Under these conditions, it is difficult to enact a vision or implement a plan. As a result, leaders cannot rely exclusively on forecasting, planning, and strategy development in Type III territory.

Meaning matters. Because organizations are ambiguous and environments uncertain, meaning is as important as planning. In Type III territory, leaders need not just facts, data, and logical reasoning but also sense-making. From a Type I or II perspective, the meaning that leaders create can appear to be little more than myths or rationalizations.[2] But it is meaning that enables understanding and action in ambiguous environments.

As unsettling as Type III territory may seem, boards should expend the effort to become more at home here because this is where ideas and plans take shape in organizations. The risks are great only when trustees inhabit this territory passively, or try to conquer it with Type I and II approaches. Familiarity with a Type III mental map, however, actually makes generative governing conceivable.

---

[2]Most people are familiar with the misuses of sense-making, where a personal sense of things *ignores* available knowledge. This is common enough, and explains why investors regularly make foolish decisions (Fuerbringer, 1997), why parents wrongly associate hyperactivity in children with excessive sugar intake (Kolata, 1996), or why members of a sect cling stubbornly to the conviction that their deceased leader will return as the Messiah (Gonzalez, 2003). As a Yale psychologist observed, "People's need to make sense of the world is so much stronger than their commitment to factual realities. Facts are easier to rearrange than their needs are" (Gonzalez, 2003).

RECOGNIZING GENERATIVE LANDMARKS

Type I and II work comes to the board at routine intervals (for example, annual budget or audit cycles) or at logical milestones (for example, transition to a new CEO or when the major goals of a strategic plan have been achieved). But how do trustees and executives know when to create a new sense of things? They can look for *generative landmarks*, *embedded issues*, and *"triple-helix" situations*.

Generative Landmarks

Several characteristics of an issue can serve as landmarks, signaling that an occasion for generative governing might be at hand:

- *Ambiguity.* There are, or could be, multiple interpretations of what is really going on and what requires attention and resolution.
- *Saliency.* The issue, however defined, means a great deal to a great many, especially influential people or important constituencies.
- *Stakes.* The stakes are high because the discussion does or could invoke questions of core values and organizational identity.
- *Strife.* The prospects for confusion and conflict and the desire for consensus are high.
- *Irreversibility.* The decision or action cannot be easily revised or reversed, due as much or more to psychological than financial commitments.

If most or all of these landmarks are present, trustees should probably work in the generative mode.

Embedded Issues

The absence of these landmarks, however, does not guarantee there is no generative work to do. As the examples in Exhibit 6.3

EXHIBIT 6.3   EMBEDDED GENERATIVE ISSUES

In these slightly disguised examples, boards uncovered the generative dimension of what were apparently technical issues. Rather than approving management *solutions,* they worked with management to understand and make sense of the *problem.*

- At a social service organization, the stated problem was voluntary turnover of staff. The technical solution proposed was to increase compensation. The board discussed the pluses and minuses of various pay plans—across-the-board versus merit pay, signing bonuses versus retention bonuses, individual rewards versus group rewards. But after deliberating in a generative mode, the problem turned out to be how to create a "great place to work" for professional staff. In the end, quality of work life, not money, was the decisive factor.
- At an independent school (grades 7–12), the stated problem was the need to hire additional psychologists to meet increased student demand for counseling. The board focused on budgetary implications and data on students: counselor ratios at peer institutions. But after more deliberation, staff and board constructed a new version of the problem: whether the school could deliver an intense intellectual experience that did not exacerbate student stress. Parental expectations, and to a lesser extent, overcrowded facilities, and not more counselors, ultimately proved to be the critical variables.
- The "problem" for one museum was the opportunity to purchase a prized (and expensive) work of art. In addition to cost, the board considered strategic priorities for the collections and the competitive consequences of foregoing the purchase. But after more deliberation, the board decided the key question was whether the museum's primary objective was to own art or display art. Based on that discussion, the board and the CEO eventually decided not to acquire the masterpiece.

illustrate, boards also need to find embedded issues—the generative elements of what appear, at first glance, to be technical or strategic questions. Because some signs are clear and others are obscure, trustees and executives need to decide first which issues are, in fact, generative. They have to observe the governing terrain carefully.

Spotting "Triple-Helix" Situations

Trustees and executives also need to be alert to "triple-helix" situations. Richard Lewontin coined this phrase to encourage people to look beyond the influence of genetics in explaining human behavior (2000). Rather than focus only on DNA (with its double helix), he urged, metaphorically, that people consider the influence of the "triple helix": the interaction of genes, organisms, and environment (Lewontin, 2000). Similarly, trustees and executives will encounter triple-helix issues that require fiduciary, strategic, and generative considerations (see examples in Exhibit 6.4).

EXHIBIT 6.4   TRIPLE-HELIX ISSUES

The Boston Museum of Fine Arts (MFA) decided to loan 21 Monet masterpieces to the Bellagio Casino in Las Vegas (Edgers, 2004).

- Type I Governance: Are the paintings travel-worthy? What are the insurance and security arrangements? Are there any bequest-related restrictions on travel or venues? How long a loan period? How much will Bellagio pay? How and where will the MFA's name appear?
- Type II Governance: Will the absence of the Monets affect MFA patronage? How will association with Bellagio and Las Vegas affect the MFA's image and reputation? Should the MFA sponsor "tie-in" events in Boston or Las Vegas? What can the MFA accomplish with the income from Bellagio?

- Type III Governance: What will we do (or not do) if the price is right? Should we loan art to the highest bidder? Should we display art where the masses already are? Do MFA masterworks "belong" in neon-light, pop-culture, for-profit venues? How conservative or iconoclastic an institution do we wish to be?

In a controversial effort to increase its national ranking, Vanderbilt University decided to make special efforts to recruit and retain more Jewish students (Golden, 2002).

- Type I Governance: Is this legal? How much will the proposed recruitment effort, academic programs, personnel, and facilities cost?
- Type II Governance: Will this tactic work? Where are our comparative advantages and disadvantages? Who are our chief competitors in this market? How will other constituencies react? Will Jewish students be comfortable here?
- Type III Governance: Will we be contributing to stereotyping, to diversity, or both? Is this exploitative or mutually beneficial? Is this part of the university's "elite strategy" consistent with the university's core values? Why do we want to climb the academic "food chain?"

Learning to spot these issues is more a matter of cultivating awareness than instituting procedures. Trustees need not make a detailed analysis of every agenda item to ensure that generative issues are not camouflaged as fiduciary and strategic matters. Explicit acknowledgement that some issues benefit from deliberation in three modes can, by itself, encourage more mindful deliberation. It may entail, however, changes in the board's norms for discussions. For some trustees, shifting from one mode to another may seem disruptive, or "paralysis by analysis." Others might appreciate such dexterity, but rely on a single "gifted" trustee to show the way. The most effective boards will be alert to the possibility of triple-helix issues, but without a penchant to find them at every turn.

WORKING AT THE BOUNDARY

If one wanted to create an environment hostile to generative thinking, the typical boardroom would be a good start. It isolates trustees from cues and clues, features only information that is already framed, makes debate about the frames off limits, and discourages encounters with outsiders that inspire generative thinking. In contrast, successful leaders are *expected* to leave the executive suite. The literature on leadership regularly recounts how, for instance, CEOs gain powerful insights from open forums with hourly workers, chance encounters with customers, or visits abroad to companies in their industry. This way of learning and leading has even earned its own acronym: MBWA, management by wandering around. Of course, for most executives, "governing by wandering around" would be a waking nightmare, with trustees on self-chartered expeditions randomly inspecting the quality of facilities, the accuracy of data, or the competency of staff. A far better approach for executives, trustees, *and* generative governing has boards start and end in the boardroom, but also work at two boundaries: at the internal border between the board and the organization, and at the external one between the board and the wider environment (see examples at Exhibit 6.5).

Working at the Internal Boundary

Work at the internal boundary gives trustees unfiltered access to the organizational stimuli that provoke generative thinking. Because the aim is to increase exposure to cues and clues (and not enforce compliance with strategies and policies), trustees need no checklist or agenda to follow. The objective is not to

EXHIBIT 6.5   BOARDS AT THE BOUNDARIES

External boundaries. The board of a 50-year-old social service agency in Florida was inclined to reclaim the organization's long-abandoned heritage as a community organizer and simultaneously deemphasize clinical therapy as a strategic priority. In order to understand the implications of this shift, the board conducted a series of site visits to organizations in the Northeast and Midwest that had followed a similar course. Three "learning groups" of trustees and staff visited three sites, talked to families served by the agency, had lengthy dinners with trustees of the host organizations, and conferred with agency executives to understand the challenges that the new approach presented with respect to finances, government contracts, program evaluation, and professional personnel. Each "learning group" arrived with a "learning agenda." The trustees returned home, more committed to the new approach, wiser about the questions to ask and the problems to anticipate.

Internal boundaries. On the eve of a five-year strategic planning process, and at the president's suggestion, the board of trustees and the department chairs at a prestigious independent college convened for a retreat. In order to better understand each other's perspective, both groups first met separately to answer questions about the other. The *faculty* was asked four questions:

1. What is the principal reason trustees agree to serve on the board?
2. What is most rewarding and most challenging about being a trustee here?
3. If you could change one thing about the board, what would it be?
4. How could the board help you be more effective?

   The trustees were asked parallel questions about the faculty. After an hour, the groups discussed the responses and learned what each did and did not understand about the other. Later in the day, mixed groups of trustees and faculty worked to define the key elements of "a successful education" at the college from an assigned perspective (for example, as students, faculty, parents, and alumni). With enriched perspectives, trustees (and faculty) were more astute sense-makers—as demonstrated the next day, when mixed groups were asked to identify "the most important questions that need to be addressed to ensure the institution's academic excellence." The exercise produced one of the most critical outcomes of sense-making and one of the most important contributions trustees can make: better questions than ever.

---

focus on selected issues, but to see what comes into focus, much as one might meander through a city or countryside to learn more about a foreign culture. It is important to observe and to converse; it is also useful to deviate, now and then, from the routes designated by travel guides. There are countless ways for trustees to do this work: attend routine occasions such as student orientations at a college or tours at a museum, volunteer as tutors or mentors at a social-service organization, talk with staff over cafeteria lunches or at special events about what they find fulfilling at work, and so on. When an important governing decision is at hand, trustees can engage in more formal consultations as well. But, in general, the harder it is for trustees to explain what they are looking for, the better the chances are that encounters along the boundary will enable generative thinking. The goal is exposure, not inspection.

Because it ultimately enables *group* decision making, trustees should do boundary work in groups. In Type III deliberations, board members generate different insights and discern different patterns by reflecting *collectively* on shared experiences. Discussions enable the interplay of different impressions, frames, and perspectives; this then moves trustees from shared *experience* to shared *meaning* and, ultimately, to a commitment to act on that shared meaning. Because this sequence of events has such consequence, trustee work at the boundary should include the

CEO and other staff. To do so underscores that this is collaborative, not evaluative, work and, more important, equips executives as well as trustees to engage in generative deliberation together.

Even so, many executives are likely to worry about trustees "on the loose" along the organization's internal boundary. Among other apprehensions, CEOs fear trustees will send or receive the wrong message, make inappropriate promises or threats, proffer dangerous ideas based on random observations, or mistake gossip for gospel. But CEOs run a far bigger risk by confining trustees to the boardroom. Deprived of shared experiences with staff and blind to the organization's indigenous culture, cues, and clues, trustees will *still* try to make sense of the organization. In the absence of other ways to see things, board members will, naturally enough, resort to the frames of their own profession. (This is why some trustees implore staff to "run this place like a business" and others urge executives to "think like a lawyer," and why CEOs become exasperated as a result.) Such a collection of imported frames can sometimes enrich an organization's perspective. But sense-making also needs to start at home, with trustees and executives able to convert shared experiences into shared meaning.

Many trustees (and CEOs) will find this proposal for internal boundary work impractical, if not inconceivable. Who has the time? What is the purpose? If we cannot trust our CEO to keep us informed, we should get a new one. Yet this is exactly how most trustees prepare for any important decision in "real life." It is why they use MBWA at work, "walk the factory floor," keep a finger on the organization's pulse, "kick the tires" on major purchases, or linger at their children's schools and summer camps. While time at the boundary, especially without tightly programmed activity, may *seem* unproductive, it is, in fact, integral to responsible decision making. As Yogi Berra commented, "You can observe a lot just by watching."

Working at the External Boundary

At the external boundary, trustees can find two other important sense-making resources: *generative occasions* and *alternative frames.*

As guardians of the mission that informs strategy, and as keepers of the strategy that guides operations, boards typically *preserve* the organization's frames rather than search for new ones. But when trustees cling to old frames, they close their organizations to new purposes, possibilities, and pathways. Unless they can consider their current goals and purposes through new frames or in contrast to alternative goals, boards really have no way of judging them. To guard against such myopia, CEOs use professional conferences, informal conversations with peers, and even board meetings[3] to find alternative frames and appropriate occasions for generative thinking.

For trustees, meeting with other boards can be a good point of departure for external boundary work. The agenda might center around common concerns: for example, increased commercialization, competition with for-profits, or changes in government policy. Boards can also discuss trusteeship, for example: What have we learned about leadership transition, critical success factors of a strategic plan, or capital campaigns? Some trustees may fear that these exchanges will only heighten the frustrations they feel in their own board room. One board is trouble enough. Why ask for more? But this frustration often arises when trustees are quarantined from conversations with

---

[3]See Chapter 2 for a discussion of board meetings as sense-making occasions for executives.

peers that would trigger interesting and consequential deliberation. Exchanges across external boundaries are more likely to
ease than compound the frustration.

Boards need not meet only with other boards. University
trustees could meet with the CEOs of companies that employ
the lion's share of the school's graduates or with the superin-
tendents of feeder school districts. Hospital trustees could meet
with third-party payers or with agencies that rate or accredit
health care facilities. Trustees could meet with influential funders or collaborators to learn how external stakeholders see the
larger environment. After these discussions, trustees are virtually
compelled to ask each other a generative question: "What do
you make of this?" As zoologist Louis Agassiz once remarked,
"Fish never discover water." Thus, external boundary work provides not only exposure to new frames but new occasions for
generative deliberation.

Internal and external boundary work is preparation for governing, not governing per se. As a result, boards should not try
to bleed grand generative breakthroughs—with profound implications for mission, strategy, and problem solving—out of every
journey to the boundary. Working and learning at the boundary may be one of the best uses of "down time" and one of the
best ways to prepare for important decisions, some not yet even
visible on the horizon. "Just-in-time inventory" may be efficient; "just-in-time knowledge" is dangerous.

LOOKING BACK: THE FUTURE
IN THE REARVIEW MIRROR

Exploring the past is one of the most important ways of getting to the future. Boards regularly examine the *fiduciary* past
through a variety of processes—from straightforward external

audits to more complex processes like Total Quality Management—to detect mistakes and misdeeds. Trustees examine the *strategic* past via "dashboards," benchmarks, and scorecards, as well as official progress reports. But in both cases, the past comes to the board compressed, aggregated, and prefabricated. Rather than working with management to create the story line, the board listens while management relates the story. For generative governance, boards need to use the past to make sense of options for the future. The key tools for this work are *retrospective questioning* and *dominant narratives.*

Most board members can dutifully recite the institution's strategic priorities for the next three to five years, but few can explain the institution's successes or setbacks over the past three to five years. Yet constructing explanations about past performance often yields new strategies, insights, or innovations. Useful explanations start with questions that uncover unrecognized strengths, unnoticed flaws, and incipient patterns:

- Why was the college able to increase dramatically both the quantity and quality of applicants without additional offers of financial aid?
- Why did the aquarium fail to fulfill strategic priorities of advocacy and education?
- How did the school achieve national recognition in the sciences when that was not an explicit element of the formal long-range plan?
- Why does the organization's staff, board, and clientele remain homogeneous despite an explicit and pervasive commitment to diversity?
- What is the most important problem we tackled in the last year? What was the most important lesson we learned in the process?

Questions like these, some about triumphs, others about dis-appointments, help the board develop a "product line" that takes the form of new solutions and strategies based on new insights about past performance. These are not questions that trustees pose to management as points of information, but rather questions that trustees and executives explore together to gain understanding.

A second retrospective technique produces not a product line but a story line: a narrative that points to a new sense of the institution's identity, which then influences changes or refinement in mission, strategies, and programs. Those who construct the organization's dominant narrative are powerful on two counts. As we discussed in the last chapter, the narrator traces an organizational trajectory, one that starts in a particular past and therefore leads to a particular future. (When people are plotting trajectories, they make statements like "Ever since *a*, we've always been about *b*, which means now we need to *c*.") But these narrators also have power because others often hear a dominant narrative as a strict account of facts, and not as one subjective formulation of what those facts and events *mean*. As a result, the narrative often goes unquestioned. Under these conditions, a dominant narrative—not trustees and executives—governs the organization.

In Type III governance, trustees and executives consider, debate, and commit to a dominant narrative, especially at moments of confusion and ambiguity (see the examples in Exhibit 6.6). They create an "organizational saga . . . a unified set of publicly expressed beliefs about the [organization] that (a) is rooted in history, (b) claims unique accomplishment, and (c) is held with sentiment" by members of the group (Clark, 1972). When trustees and executives work on the saga together, the result is not only compelling, but also legitimate.

EXHIBIT 6.6   DOMINANT NARRATIVES

Some retrospective deliberation creates a new dominant narrative that, in turn, informs the mission and strategies of the organization:

The managers of a nonprofit family counseling agency were looking for a strategy to cope with a highly competitive environment. New managed-care health insurance plans jeopardized smaller providers like them. Although they had recently seen themselves as a highly professional, clinically oriented mental health institution, their strategy work led them to recover an earlier past: a time when they did not "treat" families with therapy but when they "strengthened" families through a wide variety of community organizing, educational, and recreational programs. They changed their dominant narrative from a story about excellence in clinical services to one about community building and family strengthening. Without this narrative, they could not have embraced a strategy that called for abandoning much of their clinical work; it would not have made sense.

A public college once renowned for attracting high-performing students had long seen itself as "the poor man's Harvard." More recently, however, the school was attracting mostly academic low achievers, including nonnative English speakers who graduated from troubled high schools. Preserving the "Harvard narrative" implied a future course of action: discourage subpar students and somehow find a new generation of academic superstars. Instead, the president and faculty developed a new "history," where the university had always been a "school for underdogs." In light of this, the school recommitted to serve disadvantaged students as an essential part of its mission.

DELIBERATING AND DISCUSSING DIFFERENTLY

To lighten their load before climbing the generative curve, boards can start by jettisoning *Robert's Rules of Order* and its associated habits of mind and behavior. Together, they promote a discourse of logic, analysis, and formal argument that literally enables boards to reach resolution. This discourse may help trustees make the soundest decision, choose the most attractive option, or chart the best course, all while preserving order in the boardroom. But none of this facilitates Type III governance, where the goal is to frame decisions and choices, not make them. For Type III work, trustees need to occasionally suspend the rules of rational discourse and promote robust dialogue about generative ideas.

The Cardinal Rule: Suspend the Rules

Type III deliberation demands everything most board protocols discourage and trustees often dread. Many of us have been socialized to rely on rational discourse in the workplace. To "think like a manager" means to think rationally. And because governing has increasingly been seen as a managerial activity, focused on Type I and II work, to think like a trustee also means to think like a manager. But if managers think like managers, why do organizations also need trustees to think like managers? And if orderly, highly rational discourse is all organizations need, then why don't leaders work that way? In fact, leaders are more apt to urge that colleagues "think outside the box" than adhere to *Robert's Rules.* And so should trustees, if they want to practice generative governance.

As organizational theorists Cohen and March have argued, the ground rules of rational deliberation help people decide the best route to an agreed-upon goal (1974). In Type III mode, trustees aim to find goals. Deliberations should have the feel and flow of an off-site retreat rather than a typical board meeting; the *modus operandum* should resemble colleagues at a think tank. While not abandoning logic and analysis, boards in Type III mode use what Cohen and March call "playfulness," a "tempo-

rary relaxation of the rules" (1974) that encourages experimentation but "acknowledges reason." Admittedly, this is a difficult
pill for most trustees (and executives) to swallow. Yet playfulness
helps people envision new possibilities, patterns, problems, and
aspirations. In contrast, "a strict insistence on purposes, consis-
tency, and rationality limits [an organization's] ability to find
new purposes." When it comes to generative governing and formal discourse, the fewer the rules, the better the chances for
generative insights.

Our own deliberations for this book demanded the type of
playfulness that boards need in Type III. Because we were
attempting to understand board problems anew—rather than
simply choose the best available solutions—we could not rely
on formal, cost–benefit analysis or strict logic. Instead, we played
with devices like the "no-board scenario." By asking trustees
and executives to think about what would happen to nonprofit
organizations *without* boards, we and they were able to think,
unencumbered by received wisdom, about the value boards add.
Playing with this formulation then triggered the "no-organization
scenario," where we asked practitioners to imagine what *trustees*
would lose if their *organizations* ceased all operations for several
years. The goal of an exercise like this is to understand familiar
challenges in new ways.

Since playfulness suspends the rules, no one should be surprised that there are no rules for playfulness. It is truly a habit
of mind. But unlike vague exhortations to "think out of the
box," playfulness offers a technology of sorts—four conditions
that favor generative thinking:

Assume action informs goals rather than vice versa. Boards are devoted
to the proposition that thinking precedes doing: Trustees set

missions, which management carries out; boards develop strategies, which staff implement. But goals do not just guide actions in a linear fashion. In fact, goals frequently emerge from action. As a result, rather than using the organization's stated goals and strategies to guide action, trustees can reflect on actions as a way to discover goals and strategies. If what we do as an organization is what we are, then who are we? So instead of asking, for example, what the mission implies for the budget, trustees could ask what the budget reveals about the mission. Similarly, a board could treat a search for a new CEO as a way to reveal actual organizational goals rather than as a means to match espoused goals to a new leader (Birnbaum 1988b). Based on which candidates appeal to the search committee and why, what can be gleaned about the organization?

Consider counterfactuals and hypotheticals. By considering even improbable scenarios, boards can often make better sense of their aspirations and situations. For instance, a board and staff prone to self-pity about the "strings" attached to government money explored a hypothetical: "What if all the government funds we now received came instead from an endowment that we controlled?" Reflecting on this, some discovered that they actually valued their government funders as agents of accountability; they hassled the organization, but they also challenged the staff and board to perform better.

Similarly, on another board, a trustee committee on strategy asked: "Do we suffer the defects of our virtues?" This question provoked an assessment of the weaknesses rooted in the organization's strengths. In other cases, trustees have clarified the organization's core values by asking: What if we were organized as a for-profit entity? What is profitable but not suitable? Why do we not simply admit the wealthiest students or patients? Boards were not treating these questions as options, but as devices for understanding their organizations.

Treat intuition as actuality. Boards should not govern by hunch, but neither should they underestimate the value of intuition and inklings as launch pads for productive and consequential deliberations. By letting indistinct ideas into the boardroom, trustees can discover new directions. For example, one nonprofit board deliberately tried to envision the organization's future based on strong, but unsubstantiated, hunches that management and trustees had about the next five to ten years. Along the way, the institution discovered some new "threads" (for example, "virtual" science laboratories, and global accreditation in health care and higher education) to pull into the future.

Pose catalytic questions that invite creativity, exploration, and do not depend largely on data and logic to answer. For example:

- What three adjectives or short phrases best characterize this organization?
- What will be most strikingly different about this organization in five years?
- What do you hope will be most strikingly different about this organization in five years?
- On what list, which you could create, would you like this organization to rank at the top?
- Five years from today, what will this organization's key constituents consider the most important legacy of the current board?
- What will be most different about the board or how we govern in five years?

- How would we respond if a donor offered a $50M endowment to the one organization in our field that had the best idea for becoming a more valuable public asset?
- How would we look as a take over target by a potential or actual competitor?
- If we could successfully take over another organization, which one would we choose and why?
- What has a competitor done successfully that we would not choose to do as a matter of principle?
- What have we done that a competitor might not do as a matter of principle?
- What headline would we most/least like to see about this organization?
- What is the biggest gap between what the organization claims it is and what it actually is?

Promoting Robust Dialogue

There is no one right answer to an adaptive problem, and no correct generative insight. But there *are* plenty of bad ones. In Type III governing, trustees must spot and scrap banal, incoherent, and misguided notions and cultivate inspired, resonant, and fertile ideas instead. To tell one from another, trustees need to probe, test, and debate generative propositions. For many trustees, this is a challenge. Too many value harmony over productivity and congeniality over candor. But the very point of Type III governing is to delve deeply into sensitive subjects: the organization's "politics and religion," as reflected in its values, beliefs, and aspirations. As a result, trustees need to promote robust dialogue right where both the stakes and anxieties are high.

As a first step, boards need to preserve civility but curb the dysfunctional politeness and "groupthink" (Janis, 1982) that chill generative thinking.[4] Groupthink theory holds that unless *one* trustee raises doubts, *no* trustees raise doubts. In such an environment, trustees often just listen, sometimes carefully, sometimes inattentively as management conducts all of the organization's generative work. The trustees' silence equals acceptance, a tacit signal that management, or a board committee, "got it right." Meanwhile, the most important question goes unaddressed: "Did management, or the trustee committee, get the right *it*?" Worse, trustees may even be pleased with the apparent consensus. After all, great minds think alike, right?

Wrong. Type III governance posits that great minds think differently, and that discussions are enriched by multiple perspectives. (Otherwise, a board with a few like-minded members would suffice.) The most productive Type III deliberations have the flavor of a lively case-based discussion at, say, a law school or business school. Early parts of the conversation concern what is at issue and what is at stake—how the group defines and frames the problem(s). As the dialogue continues and potential actions are proposed, the participants welcome, and discussion leaders cultivate, different points of view and constructive criticisms, usually through questions. "Who sees the situation differently?" "What are we missing?" "How does the situation look from the vantage point of the constituents most affected by the decision at hand?" "What problems might the proposed solutions create?" "What is the best possible outcome?" "What is the worst-case scenario?" "What is the next question we should discuss?" No one expects instant agreement; everyone expects to appreciate more deeply the complexities of the situation.

---

[4]Chapter 7 describes how norms of diligence can offset the problems of excessive congeniality.

A center weight of opinion usually coalesces, though often different from the sense of the group that might have been revealed by a poll taken *before* the discussion. This is as it should be. If no one's opinion ever changes, why have discussions at all? In short, the process reveals the "collective mind" of the board and senior staff. (Exhibit 6.7 describes two real-life, slightly masked examples where the collective mind of a board was activated.) The practices suggested in Exhibit 6.8 promote conditions that are conducive to robust discussion, enable broad participation, and make discussion of generative issues everyone's work. The board moves from "dis-sensus" to consensus, airing different views so the group does not commit prematurely or preemptively to one alternative without consideration of others. Group norms stress individual preparation for collective deliberations, so that trustees come to discussions with a sense (rather than a fixed position) of what is important or worrisome. By lowering the barrier to entry in generative dialogue, boards can raise the quality of discourse.

EXHIBIT 6.7   ENGAGING THE "COLLECTIVE MIND"

Leadership Transition. With nearly a year's notice, and after consultation with the Executive Committee, the CEO informed the board of plans to retire. After some laudatory comments from trustees, and by prior arrangement with the executive committee, the CEO then exited the room. Every trustee was asked to construct two questions: one that a wise board should ask of a finalist for the presidency of the organization, and the other, that a wise finalist for the presidency would ask of the board.

The board was divided into six groups, each with four members. Each trustee's proposed questions were shared within the group, which then had to choose (or compose) the single best question the board and the candidate respectively could ask. The board, as a whole, gathered briefly to hear the proposed questions. The small groups then reconvened, this time charged to develop persuasive answers, both as a candidate and as a board, to questions posed by other groups. Thirty minutes later the board reassembled to hear the answers.

In the end, the board had better questions to ask (for example, "If you were CEO of our archrival, what would you do to most effectively compete against us?"), and better answers to questions that candidates might pose (for example, "What made the previous CEO so successful?"). Moreover, the exercise clarified the challenges that the organization faced, the leadership skills that were needed, and the expectations that candidates would have of the board. In the process, the viewpoint of every single board member was expressed, and every trustee was intellectually and psychologically engaged in the process.

Capital Campaign. In the context of the organization's overall strategic plan, trustees were asked in advance to anonymously identify possible priorities for a capital campaign. The results of the survey were presented to the board and, as appropriate, consolidated. The list of twelve priorities or needs was longer than even the most ambitious campaign could support. At this point, each trustee received five $20 bills in play money (with the picture of the incumbent president on one side, and an iconic institutional facility on the other side). Four bills were green, one was red. The red bill was "negative money," a way to signal opposition to a proposed initiative. There were twelve "ballot boxes," each labeled with a possible campaign priority. Trustees could put all their money on one priority or allocate the currency across several.

The atmosphere was animated; some trustees good-naturedly lobbied others. A few tried to create a secondary market to exchange red and green money. No one was on the sidelines, and everyone's vote mattered. The results held a few surprises. A proposed new facility and beautification of the institution's grounds, which a few vociferous trustees had strongly championed, actually garnered little support. In addition, an idea that emerged from one response to the survey, but was nowhere in the formal strategic plan, catapulted to the top of the list. The institution decided that the highest priority was a "jump start, raise it fast, spend it fast," fund that would generate momentum, excitement, and energy in a way that gifts to endowment and long-term projects could not.

EXHIBIT 6.8   TECHNIQUES FOR ROBUST
DISCUSSIONS

The techniques described here provide a "starter kit" for boards unaccustomed to trustee deliberations that are highly participative and relatively spontaneous. While they may strike some trustees as "parlor games," many boards, habituated to formal discussions, have used these devices fruitfully to acclimate to a different approach. As the board becomes more experienced and comfortable with the generative mode, there will be less need for such "contrivances;" robust discussions will occur more naturally.

Silent Starts. Prior to the *start* of a major discussion, but with advance notice, set aside two minutes for each trustee to anonymously write on an index card the most important question the board and management should consider relevant to the issue at hand. Collect and randomly redistribute the cards. Ask a trustee to read his or her card aloud, and then invite everyone with a card that has a similar question to do the same. Tally the numbers. Continue until all cards have been read aloud. Identify the question(s) most important to the most trustees *and* any question that, once raised, even if only by one person, the board now recognizes as crucial.

One Minute Memos. At the *conclusion* of a major discussion, reserve two to three minutes for trustees to write down, anonymously or not, what they would have said next had there been time to continue the discussion. Collect the cards for review by the board chair and CEO. No trustee suffers the pain of an undelivered remark or unstated concern, and the organization's leadership no longer wonders what remained on the trustees' minds.

Future Perfect History. In breakout groups, develop a narrative that explains in the future perfect tense how the organization moved from its current state to an envisioned state. For example, five years from now the college will have achieved greater student and faculty diversity as a result of taking the following steps. Compare the story lines for common pathways as well as attractive, imaginative "detours."

Counterpoints. Randomly designate two to three trustees to make the most powerful counterarguments to initial recommendations or an embryonic consensus. Or ask management to present the strongest case against (as well as for) a staff recommendation.

Role Plays. Ask subsets of the board to assume the perspective of different constituent groups likely to be affected by the issue at hand. How would these stakeholders frame the issue and define a successful outcome? What would each group regard as a worst-case scenario? The role play would be enhanced if all trustees were asked in advance to meet informally with one or two such constituents.

Breakouts. Small groups expand available "air time," ease participation by reticent trustees, and counter "groupthink." On topics of substantive, strategic, or symbolic significance, small groups, even within 30 minutes, can raise important considerations. Do we have the right questions? How else might the issue be framed? What values are at stake? What would constitute a successful outcome? In plenary session, the board can search for consensus, conflicts, and a better understanding of the matter at hand.

Simulations. Trustees can simulate some decisions, not to second-guess the decision but to provoke discussion about the trade-offs that management faces. For example, trustees of an independent college or school could review the redacted applications of the next 20 students who would have been admitted last year if the institution opted for larger enrollments and additional revenues rather than greater selectivity and higher quality.

Surveys. The board can administer an anonymous survey prior to discussion of a major issue. For instance:

- "What should be atop the board's agenda next year?"
- "What are the most attractive, least attractive, most worrisome aspects of the proposed strategic plan?"
- "What external factors will most affect the organization in the next year?"
- "What are we overlooking at the organization's peril?"
- "What is the most valuable step we could take to be a better board?"

The answers would be collated for board discussion. The discussion would start not by a response to the first person to speak on an issue, but by an analysis of the collective responses.

MIND THE MODE

Boards are expected to monitor organizational performance and hold management accountable. No notion of trusteeship excludes this basic responsibility. The tools and techniques for assessing Type I performance include audits, management letters, financial statements, accreditation reports, and compliance reviews by government agencies. In Type II, as we noted in Chapter 4, boards assess institutional performance in the context of strategic goals, using processes like *The Balanced Scorecard* (Kaplan and Norton, 1996), benchmarking (Watson, 1993), dashboards (Chait, Holland, and Taylor, 1996), strategic indicators (Taylor and Massy, 1996), or best practices. Type III governing requires a different approach: Trustees and executives reflect on their ability to effectively do generative work together.

Trustees and executives can use this reflection to ensure that they are doing the deliberate generative work of governance as leadership, and not inadvertently succumbing to governance by default. Some first steps might be to:

- Compare recent and past agendas. Do we do more generative work now?
- Review, over the course of a year, where and when trustees worked at the boundaries.
- Consider how often the board spotted or missed "triple helix" issues in the last year or two.
- Survey trustees on whether the climate for robust discussion has improved or deteriorated.
- With input from senior staff, and perhaps even key constituents, spend a couple of hours a year as a board addressing questions like these:

- Have we clarified (or muddled) organizational values and beliefs?
- Have we clarified (or muddled) the organization's vision?
- Have we discovered new ends as we have modified means?
- Have we reframed important problems?
- What do we know now about governing that we did not know before?
- What did we once know about the organization that is no longer true?
- What did we once know to not be true about the organization that now is?
- Where did we miss the landmarks of generative issues and why?

If boards in Type II mode need to understand strategy, then boards in Type III mode need a strategy for understanding. The exercises and questions presented here will help boards assess how successful that strategy has been.

THE PAYOFFS

To add the generative mode to the board's repertoire, and to do that work well, trustees have to learn new ways that disrupt old habits. (See Exhibit 6.9 for a comparison of the three modes.) The transition may be awkward and boards may be self-conscious. There may even be some initial awkwardness as the board becomes comfortable with a new approach. Change is almost never without stress. Organizational theorist Edgar Schein (1993) suggested that significant change occurs only when anxiety over the failure to change supercedes the anxiety associated with change. For instance, technophobes usually relent only when the

EXHIBIT 6.9   THREE TYPES OF GOVERNANCE: DISTINCTIVE CHARACTERISTICS

	Type I Fiduciary	Type II Strategic	Type III Generative
Nature of organizations	Bureaucratic	Open System	Nonrational
Nature of leadership	Hierarchical	Analytical/visionary	Reflective learners
Board's central purpose	Stewardship of tangible assets	Strategic partnership with management	Source of leadership for organization
Board's core work	Technical: oversee operations, ensure accountability	Analytical: shape strategy, review performance	Creative: discern problems, engage in sense-making
Board's principal role	Sentinel	Strategist	Sense maker
Key question	What's wrong?	What's the plan?	What's the question?
Problems are to be	Spotted	Solved	Framed
Deliberative process	Parliamentary and orderly	Empirical and logical	Robust and sometimes playful
Way of deciding	Reaching resolution	Reaching consensus	Grappling and grasping
Way of knowing	It stands to reason	The pieces all fit	It makes sense
Communication with constituents	Limited, ritualized to legitimate	Bilateral, episodic to advocate	Multilateral, ongoing to learn
Performance metrics	Facts, figures, finances, reports	Strategic indicators, competitive analysis	Signs of learning and discerning

fear of obsolescence or unemployment overwhelms discomfort with "new-fangled" hardware or software. Therefore, nonprofit boards hesitant to open a "third front" of trusteeship—the generative mode—should first recall that the status quo imposes considerable costs, namely the irrelevance, disengagement, and underutilization of trustees, and the burden on staff to create an illusion to the contrary. When trustees operate *only* in the fiduciary and strategic modes, the board pays a steep price: problems of purpose and performance persist. The organization also incurs a substantial penalty: the board's untapped value as a source of leadership. In short, boards should not mistake a high level of comfort with a high level of performance.

By contrast, when boards develop the ability to work effectively and move appropriately *across all three modes* with a special awareness of Type III governance, there are handsome dividends for both trustees and the organization. The benefits of Types I and II governance are widely recognized and well-documented. The payoffs from the generative mode are not as broadly appreciated because fewer boards regularly practice Type III governance (see Exhibit 6.10). Nevertheless, we believe the benefits are substantial. Specifically, generative governance:

- *Empowers the board to do meaningful work.* The very nature of the generative mode prompts trustees, with management, to do the most important work of all: to frame on the front end the problematic situations that most demand organizational attention and to make sense of the organization's experiences. These are acts of leadership.
- *Engages the "collective mind."* Type III governance places a greater premium on a plurality of perspectives than on technical expertise. Rather than rely on one or two trustees

Type III trusteeship stakes new ground for governance, although what is new for boards has a familiar ring to leaders. The hallmark characteristics of the generative mode can be summarized as follows:

- *A different view of organizations.* Organizations do not travel a straight line and rational course from vision to mission to goals to strategy to execution.
- *A different definition of leadership.* Leaders enable organizations to confront and move forward on complex, value-laden problems that defy a "right" answer or "perfect" solution.
- *A different mindset.* Beyond fiduciary stewardship and strategic partnership, governance is tantamount to leadership.
- *A different role.* The board becomes an asset that creates added value and comparative advantage for the organization.
- *A different way of thinking.* Boards are intellectually playful and inventive as well as logical and linear.
- *A different notion of work.* The board frames higher-order problems as well as assesses technical solutions, and asks questions that are more catalytic than operational.
- *A different way to do business.* The board relies more on retreat-like meetings, teamwork, robust discourse, work at the organization's boundaries, and performance metrics linked to organizational learning.

to devise a technical solution or assess preconceived alternatives, the board elicits multiple viewpoints to better define the problems and better understand circumstances.

- *Enriches the board's work.* Type III governance presents a substantively and intellectually attractive agenda that transcends the maintenance of order and the extrapolation of strategy. The board has a better job, more interesting work, and a more influential role. Trustees escape the "substitute's dilemma" and derive a higher rate of return on involvement.

- *Enhances the board's value.* Type III governance emphasizes the distinctive, indispensable contributions that a board can make as a source of leadership. The board adds more value because the trustees utilize the levers of leadership—the formulation of the issues that precede the deliberations, the ideas that drive the plan, and the interpretations of the past that illuminate the present and the future.

We turn in the next chapter to how the assets of trustees can best be deployed to achieve these outcomes.

CHAPTER 7

Working Capital That Makes Governance Work

Taken together, the fiduciary, strategic, and generative modes of governing provide a fresh view of nonprofit boards that accentuates the board as a source of leadership. A new perspective on boards leads naturally to new ideas about trustees. In fact, the implications are inescapable. When we redefine the nature of governance and modify expectations for boards, we inevitably rethink the requisites for trustees. What are the most beneficial assets that trustees can contribute to make governance as leadership work? How can the untapped potential of the board be unleashed?

For years, board members were selected on the basis of certain desired traits. Because the board was a critical instrument of legitimacy, organizations usually favored trustees of social stature, moral integrity, and refined lineage. These characteristics were also a powerful predictor of another important attribute: wealth. To create a congenial and comfortable atmosphere, charitable organizations also preferred polite and proper board members. In 1971, Myles Mace described for-profit directors as "ornaments" on the corporate Christmas tree (Mace, as quoted in Lorsch and Maciver, 2000). And nonprofit boards were often no different.

With the advent of strategic planning and market-based competition, nonprofit organizations placed greater and greater emphasis on the recruitment of trustees with pertinent expertise. (See Chapter 3.) Worksheets developed by BoardSource, the Association of Governing Boards of Universities and Colleges, and other umbrella organizations invariably included a checklist of professional skills or occupational backgrounds that might be represented on the "model" board, for example, accounting, government, law, marketing, real estate, strategy, and technology (Hughes, Lakey, and Bobowick, 2000). Although the principal selection criteria for trustees shifted from characteristics toward competencies, with increased attention to demographic diversity, one criterion remained constant: the capacity for substantial philanthropy relative to one's means.

Whether focused primarily on trustees' qualities or skills (or some combination), nonprofits generally acquire, rather than develop, these assets—almost like corporations that expand by takeovers rather than by product development, or universities that "steal" star professors from the competition rather than promote from within. On the whole, boards harvest, rather than cultivate, trustees with attractive traits and talents. Second, these assets appreciate modestly, if at all. An honest, polite trustee does not become more honest and more polite. An able lawyer or banker does not become markedly more proficient. And certainly, a male or female, or black or white trustee does not become more so over time. These trustee assets resemble an investment grade bond—a reliable, steady performer with virtually guaranteed dividends, but without significant upside potential. We know what we have, and we know, more or less, what this will yield.

The analogy to financial markets has relevance because trustees can be reframed as a source of multiple forms of capital, and not merely as *pro bono* consultants to the organization. A board contributes various types of capital, and then invests those resources in the governance of the institution, ideally at a favorable rate of return to the organization. In the best cases, the capital represented by the board appreciates substantially over time. The most valuable boards contribute and invest more capital from more sources in more forms than other boards. The boards with the most capital provide the organization with a comparative edge, the ability to "outgovern" the competition, just as the most astute and industrious staff can outsmart and outwork the competition. The emphasis on capital underscores one other consideration: to generate value capital must be deployed. Money under the mattress, or boards under anesthesia, are idle capital. For the purposes of governance as leadership, trustees must be working capital. (See Exhibit 7.1, which calculates the monetary value of a board's time when we convert voluntarism into real dollars.)

When boards are conceptualized as a source of capital, money leaps to mind, and we do not underestimate the importance of financial capital. Nonprofit organizations cannot do much without money, and much of this money flows directly or indirectly from trustees. However, trustee largesse and excellent governance are not synonymous, nor does institutional wealth negate the need for an effective board. Even the most affluent nonprofits require governance.

Board members and senior staff must learn to recognize, appreciate, and capture the value of four no less crucial forms of capital, beyond money, that trustees can provide. These are intellectual, reputational, political, and social capital (see Exhibit 7.2). Each form of capital can be generated by trustees and

EXHIBIT 7.1	THE DOLLAR VALUE OF THE BOARD'S TIME

Consider the board of a college, museum, school, symphony orchestra, hospital, or regional or national social service agency. There are perhaps 30 members on the board which typically meets five times a year for eight hours at a time. Now do the math.

Assume that the trustees, mostly successful professionals or executives, earn on average $200,000 a year. At that rate, the board "burns" about $120,000 a year. Many nonprofit boards have more members and meet more often, especially in committees, or for longer periods of time. In these cases, the "billable hours" can easily exceed $150,000 annually. On elite boards, where the average annual income might be twice as much, the board's contributed services could easily exceed $300,000. If the calculation were based on the trustees' net worth, the dollar value of the board's time would soar.

For that amount of money over the course of a year, trustees would expect a lot from lawyers, accountants, consultants, or other professionals the organization retained. In this sense, most non-profit organizations leave a lot of money on the boardroom table. As fiduciaries, trustees strive to maximize the rate of return to the organization on facilities, endowment, personnel, technology, and other institutional assets. Ironically, few calibrate a rate of return on the board or even ask whether trustees represent an underutilized asset.

---

invested on the institution's behalf. And while every nonprofit board contributes some capital to the organization, sometimes unconsciously or passively (for example, the very existence of a board generates some legitimacy) and sometimes through gratis technical expertise, the strongest boards generate more capital more actively, purposefully, and productively.

The assets of a highly capitalized board should be balanced and diversified. Like a mixed-asset allocation model, the multiple forms of capital offer a template to analyze whether the board

EXHIBIT 7.2 THE FOUR FORMS OF BOARD CAPITAL

Form of Capital	Resource Optimized	Traditional Use	Enhanced Value
Intellectual	Organizational learning	Individual trustees do technical work	Board as a whole does generative work
Reputational	Organization legitimacy	Organization trades on trustees' status	Board shapes organizational's status
Political	Organizational power	External heavyweight: Trustees exercise power on the outside	Internal fulcrum: Board balances power on the inside
Social	Efficacy of the board	Trustees strengthen relationships to gain personal advantage	Trustees strengthen relationships to bolster board's diligence

has an appropriate portfolio of capital to do governance as leadership in light of the organization's needs and aims. Because the model highlights the value of other assets (for example, resourcefulness, persuasiveness, and trustworthiness), the board's attention may be redirected from narrow fiduciary matters toward other less visible, but arguably more significant, priorities. As a result, different issues (and different trustees) may become important to the board.

We now turn to the four forms of capital that boards need to develop in order to govern on a higher plane. In this context, one might think about a "capital campaign" as an effort to acquire and deploy the resources that trustees must furnish for governance to become an act of leadership.

INTELLECTUAL CAPITAL

All three modes of governance place a premium on intellectual attributes, whether technical expertise, strategic acumen, or generative ingenuity. (By contrast, affluence and pedigree are not essential to any mode.) Each mode suggests a different way to think about trusteeship and a different way to think as a trustee. In that sense, this entire book concerns intelligence. Since "wisdom" or "talent" have always been one of the trinities of trusteeship, one might reasonably ask "What's new about that?"[1]

We are not concerned here with the intellectual prowess of individual board members or a search for trustees with the most impressive IQs or SAT scores. Instead, we are concerned with intellectual capital: the "collective brainpower" that "can be put

---

[1]The standard versions of the trilogy are "work, wisdom, and wealth" and "time, talent, and treasure."

to use" (Stewart, 1997) to generate mission-critical resources. While regularly applied to both white- and blue-collar workers, the term has not been linked to boards of trustees (or corporate boards, for that matter).

Intellectual capital is *not* the sum of trustees' knowledge, any more than the intellectual capital of a law firm comprises the sum of what each attorney knows. Effective boards and successful companies require shared knowledge, or "organizational intelligence," defined by Thomas Stewart as "smart people working in smart ways" (1997). A gulf between what individuals know and what the organization knows occurs so often that the syndrome has been condensed into a popular maxim: "If IBM only knew what IBM knows." The same could be said about boards of trustees. Each trustee has a storehouse, but the board as a whole often lacks common knowledge.

As we observed about the fiduciary and strategic modes, management frequently consults board members about technical matters such as audits, investment strategies, legal questions, real estate, marketing, and competitive positioning. Do we self-insure or purchase coverage? Invest abroad or only domestically? Renovate or raze? The organization "capitalizes" on the trustees' individual talents, skills, and experiences to answer such questions. So far, so good, but not good enough.

Governance as leadership requires more than individuals with various expertise, just as orchestras require more than musicians with mastery of various instruments. There must be a shared sense of the nature of the work and enough common knowledge to do the work together. Governance as leadership flourishes when what the *board* knows informs what the *board* thinks—when the "collective brainpower" of the board enlightens the "collective mind" of the board.

This suggests that boards act as "communities of practice," creating multiple opportunities for the entire board or particular committees to pool usable knowledge and thereby learn together. (Exhibit 7.3 offers three examples of community of practice, each pegged to a particular governing mode.) Some knowledge is explicit, for instance, tactics to negotiate with a labor union or steps to accelerate construction projects. Other knowledge is tacit, like the intuition, instincts, and sixth sense that trustees access to assess people, opportunities, and trade-offs. Both "hard" and "soft" knowledge should be expressly communicated and collectively absorbed. For example, the entire board of an independent college, school, or hospital should understand why competition drives costs up, not down. The entire board of an orchestra or opera should know what motivates musicians. On every board, all trustees should know what some trustees know first-hand about the benefits and pitfalls of strategic planning. And every board should discover and discuss together the most important lessons the trustees have learned about governing over the past year.

EXHIBIT 7.3   COMMUNITIES OF PRACTICE

Leadership Transition. (Generative mode) Upon the appointment of a new president from outside the organization, the trustees of a large university considered how the board could be most helpful in the transition. Initial suggestions were to familiarize the president-designate with the organization's budget, personnel, and structure (Type I). Then, some trustees recommended that the Executive Committee meet with the new CEO to review the strategic plan and "backlogged" priorities (Type II). In the end, the board decided that the most useful step would be to have all trustees and the CEO meet for three hours to discuss, based on personal experience or second-hand accounts, the most (and least) effective ways for a new executive to enter an organization from the outside and "take charge." The upshot was a well-advised new CEO and an entire board better acquainted with the meaning and constraints of a university presidency, and more appreciative of the challenges of the office.

Development. (Strategic mode) The leadership of an organization that envisioned a capital campaign on the horizon was concerned that not all board members understood the elements of an effective program to engage stakeholders and promote philanthropic support. The Advancement Committee asked three trustees to serve on a panel, facilitated by a fourth, to talk with the board about their involvement in successful campaigns with other nonprofits. The topics included how their skills were put to use, the most valuable lesson or best practice they learned, what motivates giving, and the responsibilities they shouldered. The result was that a board, where trustees previously had different levels of familiarity and expertise with advancement, now had a shared understanding of building volunteer relationships, setting funding priorities, and conducting a campaign.

Financial Oversight. (Fiduciary mode) The board of a religiously sponsored nonprofit included many members without a financial background. As a result, relatively few trustees contributed to discussions about the organization's financial performance. In order to narrow the knowledge gap and expand participation, the trustees instituted a "Finances 101" refresher seminar, conducted by board members, just prior to receipt of the outside auditor's report. Now every member of the board, throughout the year, has a level of financial literacy sufficient to participate in fiduciary discussions about budgets, audits, and resource allocation.

Intellectual capital increases as more trustees understand more together. In turn, the organization profits far more from a knowledgeable board than from a loose federation of knowledgeable trustees. As a mental exercise, the board should periodically review an intellectual capital balance sheet that records what all trustees know now that some or all did not know—say, a year ago—about what the organization values and expresses; what constituents seek and experience; what the organization does and does not do, might or should do; and what works, what does not, and why. The threshold question then becomes not "What does *one* make of all this?" but "What do *all* make of this?"

REPUTATIONAL CAPITAL

Reputational capital, the ultimate intangible asset, can be converted into real value when "the power of a good reputation is harnessed to improve the relationships on which successful business depends" (Jackson, 2004).[2] Whether reflected in stock price or the premium offered to acquire a company, reputation enhances a company's power to price products, attract clients, and recruit personnel. A tarnished reputation, by comparison, can be lethal.

The same principles apply to nonprofits, only more so. The services and products nonprofits offer are purchased largely on faith rather than on empirical qualities or demonstrable outcomes. Consumers and donors depend heavily on the reputation of the college, clinic, or charity to make choices, whereas reputation has almost no effect on the purchase of commodities like light bulbs, eggs, and gasoline. This explains why these products frequently retail as generics or private labels. The brand name and, by extension, the reputation of the manufacturer barely matter. In contrast, it is virtually impossible to imagine a successful generic nonprofit. Armed with a strong reputation,

---

[2]Corporate balance sheets assign tangible worth to goodwill as the market value of a company's shares beyond the liquidation value of its assets.

a nonprofit will be favorably positioned to access capital markets, recruit talented staff, attract capable trustees, and engender public support. Reputation may not be everything, but whatever occupies second place ranks far behind.

Mindful of the value of reputation, nonprofits employ various techniques to enhance relationships with critical constituencies—for example, improve performance and quality, especially as perceived by critical constituencies; obtain professional accreditation or certification; assure transparency; recruit noteworthy personnel; seek positive publicity; and mount image campaigns. However, remarkably few nonprofits leverage the board's reputational capital into substantial value for the organization.

The process starts with the selection of trustees. A board cannot accumulate or expend reputational capital through a haphazard approach to recruitment. The organization should ask, "What reputation do we want to advance (or repair) with what stakeholders?" For instance, an organization with a damaged reputation may require different trustees than one with a reputation intact. Or, a low-status organization may need high-status trustees, while a high-status organization may need more worker bees than queen bees.

Nonprofits attuned to the value of a board's reputation will intentionally make appointments that cultivate a particular reputation with a particular audience. Thus, the board of a New England college appointed several distinguished scholars to underscore to faculty and students the trustees' commitment to academic quality. The board of a midwestern hospital traditionally includes clergy to convey to patients and physicians an allegiance to the precepts and ethics of the sponsoring order. (In the for-profit sector, various corporations, stained by scandal, have appointed outside directors of unassailable integrity in order to assure stockholders of the company's probity.) However adroitly accomplished, inspired appointments add only nominal value; far greater advantage arises when trustees are actively engaged on the organization's behalf. The relationships between trustee reputation and trustee engagement are illustrated in Exhibit 7.4.

Deadwood add no value; figureheads add token value. In the latter case, nonprofits exploit the "halo effect" as stakeholders transfer to the organization the legitimacy of prominent trustees. (The same principle applies in reverse: When the personal reputations of certain executives were tarnished by corporate misdeeds, many were encouraged or forced to resign from nonprofit boards to spare the organization taint by association.) The organization borrows board members' status at no cost to the trustees, a passive transaction for both parties. Of course, no-show, luminary trustees can also be a liability, especially when these "celebrities" confess to colleagues and acquain-

EXHIBIT 7.4	BRAND NAME VALUE OF BOARD MEMBERS	
Level of Trustee Engagement	**Trustee Reputation and Name Recognition**	
	High	**Low**
High	*Superstars* Marquee name, leadership role.	*Worker bees* Little or no name recognition, much sweat equity.
Low	*Figureheads* All hat, no horse. Brand equity without sweat equity.	*Deadwood* No hat, no horse, no value.

tances indifference or ignorance about the organization's purposes and performance.

Some nonprofits ask that trustees lend only a name but never a hand. Over the long run, however, a renowned roster of "nonplayers" records few victories. The rate of return on the board's reputational capital accelerates with trustee engagement. Therefore, nonprofits customarily seek 100 percent participation by trustees in the capital campaign or annual fund to symbolize the board's support for the organization and to strengthen the case to other development prospects. At a more advanced level, the worker bees and superstars publicly commend and promote the organization, visibly volunteer, and enthusiastically use the organization's services. (I have a child enrolled here. I had surgery here. I attended a support group here.)

While helpful, these measures do not leverage the trustees' reputation. More resourceful and valuable examples include:

- Trustees of a private college contact the parents of the ablest high school seniors offered admission to tout the institution, answer questions, and express a personal interest in the student. Whenever possible, the college matches the trustee's background to the student's academic interests.
- At programs for parents of prospective students, trustees—not admissions officers or the headmaster—of an independent school explain the institution's strengths, values, and benefits, and answer parents' questions.
- The board of an eminent nonprofit, widely regarded as well-governed, parlayed that feature to "trade up in the applicant pool" for a new CEO.

In all of these cases, the trustees were not just dispatched by management on tactical missions to mend or fortify relationships with a particular constituency. Rather, the board consciously and strategically decided which stakeholders were sufficiently important to the organization's future to warrant the investment of a valuable resource: the trustees' reputational capital.

Boards are uniquely situated to generate and expend reputational capital. Trustees have credibility and stature as respected citizens, prestigious professionals, objective overseers, dedicated volunteers, and generous donors. These are truly distinctive attributes and assets, especially when taken together, that are not present anywhere else in the organization, no matter how gifted the executives or staff may be.

Furthermore, as we noted in Chapter 6, board members engaged in generative governance straddle the boundary between the organization and the larger environment. In other words, trustees operate exactly where reputations are forged. As with other competitive enterprises, the winners take advantage of location, while the also-rans do not. Trustees restricted to the boardroom and isolated from the intersections of influence contribute little or no reputational capital to fuel the organization's success. So life at the organization's boundaries promises at least two advantages: more grist for generative governance and more reputational capital for the institution.

POLITICAL CAPITAL

All organizations, nonprofits no less than for-profits, are political systems where people, individually or in groups, attempt to acquire and retain control over various resources in order to pursue certain interests. In the process, conflicts arise, coalitions form, participants jockey for power, negotiations occur, compromises emerge, and decisions happen. Political capital connotes, in shorthand, the influence and leverage that people within an organization acquire and deploy to frame problems, to elevate one above others, and to promote one solution over another.

Despite noble missions, nonprofits are hardly above organizational politics. First, nonprofits are particularly pluralistic institutions with diverse parties, inside and outside the organization, that passionately pursue multiple, and often contradictory, goals. Without the common bond of a profit motive, interest groups arise, coalesce, and dissolve contingent on the issues under consideration. Second, nonprofits are not as hierarchical as corporations; most have an innate aversion to formal authority. Compared to business executives, nonprofit managers have noticeably less power. Not many can issue decrees, and far fewer can expect that any mandates will, in fact, be heeded. The autonomy of professionals (for example, physicians, musicians, professors, curators) neutralizes, or even trumps, the authority of management. Finally, participants vie over where and how decisions will be reached. Because process matters as much or more than substance, no one can easily assert the right to make a decision; authority and legitimacy are not one and the same.

To go a step further, we postulate that the political capital of the board matters most in the generative mode, where the consequences for the institution and the potential for conflict are both high. Therefore, a substantial expenditure of political capital will be necessary to encourage and prod the organization to confront generative questions many constituents would prefer to ignore. Questions of core values (Type III) will generally precipitate more intense discussion and dispute than questions of core competencies (Type II) or core budgets (Type I). Proposed departures from tradition (for example, the elimination of fraternities at a college, obstetrics at a hospital, or free admission at a museum) will almost certainly incite more ambivalence and disagreement than proposed departures from the operating budget or even the strategic plan. Granted, boards may have to expend political capital to nudge management to tackle fiduciary issues like deferred maintenance or inefficient energy systems, and strategic topics like targets of opportunity and competitive responses. On the whole, however, boards should carefully conserve political capital that can, when necessary, be judiciously deployed to frame, accentuate, and confront generative issues.

Nonprofit boards accumulate political capital principally in two ways. First, the potential to exert influence emerges from the trustees' eloquence, intelligence, expertise, prestige, and charisma. These are all means to have sway. In this sense, the board "buys" political capital through the recruitment of powerful trustees. Second, an openness to influence spawns influence and creates reciprocity of power. The board accumulates political capital when trustees are demonstrably susceptible to influence, for example, at executive sessions with the CEO, lunches with senior managers, open forums with clients, multiconstituency task forces with professional staff, focus groups with patrons, or attendance at organizational events. In this sense, the board "makes" political capital through the interplay of influence. Make or buy, the trustees' political capital enhances and balances the distribution of power available to the organization.

Traditionally, nonprofit executives harness the political capital of boards when constituents inside the organization want trustees to influence events and advocate positions outside the organization. Alert to the value of friends in high places, management may marshal the political capital of a well-connected board to lobby local or state government; to encourage favorable treatment from the media; to seek special considerations from the community or from corporations; or to persuade skeptical patrons, alumni, or donors that a controversial proposal or decision deserves support. These are the ordinary, and almost invariably fiduciary or strategic, external applications of the trustees' political capital.

Mobilization of the board's political capital inside the organization presents a somewhat different picture. Individual trustees, of course, spend political capital internally all the time, for instance, through a phone call or an aside to the CEO, a contingent pledge, a special plea, a request for information—even an arched eyebrow. When trustees act alone, executives can become confused, frustrated, and whipsawed. On occasion, a single board member with ample political capital may prevail, regardless of the merits of the argument, which only further exasperates management. At worst, the board becomes little more than a horde of lobbyists for personal preferences and pet projects; in effect, the trustees start to look and act like every other constituency.

In order to achieve an attractive rate of return on the board's political capital, nonprofit organizations must avoid the extremes. At one end of the spectrum, some CEOs question the risk/reward ratio of a board internally influential beyond the fiduciary sphere. These executives favor and design structures that preclude all but the most cursory relationships between trustees and staff or stakeholders lest board members be unduly influenced by constituents or vice versa. At the other extreme, some boards plunge headlong into the internal fray, not merely to influence events but to unilaterally impose policies, programs, and even personnel. As described in the previous chapter, a board reluctant to assert influence internally invites governance by default, and a board hell-bent on exercising formal authority and veto power at every turn produces governance by fiat. Neither extreme has much to offer.

A more balanced approach that taps the board's political capital with little risk for management and substantial advantage for the organization adheres to three guidelines. First and foremost, the board expends political capital *as a board*—the outcome of collective determination, not the exercise of personal prerogative. While inherently desirable as a means to foster cohesiveness within the board, this approach promises an even more pragmatic advantage: preservation of capital. The more that trustees act independently, the faster the board's political capital dissipates; in nonprofit boardrooms as in capital markets, institutional investors have far greater leverage than individuals.

Second, the board asserts influence primarily through mainstream processes rather than back channels. Committed to transparency and accountability, nonprofit boards must rely on legitimate means to achieve legitimate ends. We do not expect boards, or board members, to peddle influence, pursue self-interest, or negotiate secret deals. In short, nonprofits, as a matter of principle, should invest political capital in "open markets."

Third, unique among all stakeholders, the board serves as the fulcrum of organizational politics, the counterbalance to the parochial interests of other constituencies. This may, from time to time, position the board as the "loyal opposition": independent-minded, impartial, and sufficiently dedicated to the *organization's* success to stake a contrary position or make an unpopular decision. At stressful and, one hopes, rare moments like these, when the trustees decide to withdraw political capital from the board's account, surely they will cherish the value of the political capital they methodically stockpiled in calmer times.

SOCIAL CAPITAL

Few concepts are more familiar or more misunderstood than "social capital," which sociologist Douglas Massey defines as the "productive value that can be extracted from social networks and organizations" (Massey, 2002). Confusion arises when people equate *relationships* with *social capital*; these are not synonymous terms. Relationships comprise the raw material that produces social capital. For instance, a close-knit neighborhood may create a safer environment for children, or a tightly integrated professional network may facilitate the exchange of valuable information about employment opportunities or best practices.

In an organizational context, certain characteristics (for example, a sense of inclusiveness, trust, shared values, and common purpose) enable people to extract productive value from their relationships. These attributes accelerate cooperation, commitment, cohesiveness, and efficient exchange of knowledge and information which, in turn, advance purposeful activity and common enterprise. As the group strengthens these qualities, the members' productivity increases and generates tangible benefits for the organization. By contrast, members of a group without social capital are far less motivated to act productively and achieve collectively.

Boards of trustees necessarily involve social relationships, but social relationships do not necessarily produce the kind of social capital that improves board performance. On some boards, most notably Type I boards, trustees are apt to have rather tenuous and distant relationships. The formal, compartmentalized nature of the work does not foster much interaction or induce much trust among board members. On other boards, where adaptive or strategic problems are tackled together, trustees may be closer and more intact as a team. And while the latter breed may enjoy a more sociable atmosphere, no advantage accrues unless and until the rapport and connections are converted into productive assets.

Typically, trustees convert the board's social relationships into social capital that serves their own personal, professional, commercial, or political interests. On prestigious boards, some members may seek social advancement through closer ties to social elites. Pursuit of self-interest does promote personal relationships; however, the social capital generated does not directly serve the organization or benefit the board. This advantage results when trustees ask, "What can social capital do to improve the board's performance or the organization's condition?"

Most important, boards can produce social capital by changing the dominant norms, the unspoken and unwritten rules that guide trustee behavior. The norm that boards most commonly reinforce through the mechanisms of social capital is congeniality. Trustees tend to be agreeable and like-minded colleagues, desirable qualities to a point. More than occasionally, the pendulum swings too far, and some or many trustees become reticent, acquiescent adherents of an unexamined consensus and few, if any, feel answerable for organizational performance. The compliant majority typically treats critics and skeptics as troublemakers and subtly sanctions the outliers with less air time, fewer important assignments, curtailed access to critical information, and social isolation. In the end, the board lacks both robust discourse and a sense of shared responsibility, essential ingredients of governance as leadership.

This creates problems in all three modes of governance. If no one feels "licensed" to raise questions about lavish expenditures or financial shenanigans, there can be massive fiduciary failure. If trustees lack "permission" to challenge dubious assumptions or questionable strategies included in a five-year plan, the organization may falter or even fold. Just as significantly, the trustees' ability to do generative governance will be impaired, or perhaps squelched, if the board's prevalent norms discourage uninhibited conversations, alternative frames, and playful ideas.

There is an alternative. Like a top-notch management team, athletic squad, musical ensemble, or law firm, a board of trustees can translate personal relationships and mutual trust into social capital that stresses personal responsibility, collective industry, and improved performance.

Several mechanisms can lead to new norms of diligence. At a minimum, a board can develop a baseline statement of expectations for both individual trustees and the board as a whole. The value of a "code of conduct" should neither be dismissed nor overestimated. It is a point of departure. In one dramatic example, the trustees of a large nonprofit in metropolitan New York concluded at a retreat that the board's performance, based on an external evaluation and an internal self-assessment, was lackluster at best. Buoyed by the *esprit de corps* generated at the retreat, the trustees summoned the resolve to assume greater accountability and to articulate new, rigorous norms. The board then declared a sixty-day "open enrollment" period when incumbent trustees could either "re-up" under the new expectations or resign. About five of 30 members resigned, while the rest have adhered to a stiffer, self-imposed standard of performance and accountability. Attendance, engagement, and trustee satisfaction all increased significantly because the board parlayed a stronger group identity into more stringent norms and loftier internal expectations.

To further foster a norm of diligence, trustees can be placed in high-stakes environments where they may be held accountable for their performance and the organization's. These venues, as we have noted, are situated at organizational boundaries, where trustees—individually or, even better, as part of small groups—represent the board and the institution before various stakeholders. This tack recognizes an irony of governance: Boards act least like trustees when closeted together inside the boardroom and most like trustees when required to represent the organization outside the boardroom. To create and internalize a norm of diligence, trustees must leave the comfortable, secure atmosphere of the boardroom where laxity can go unremarked on, let alone challenged.

Thus, subgroups of trustees of a nationally prominent nonprofit personally visited with foundation officers to explain the organization's recent setbacks, to outline a course of action, and to request (ultimately, successfully) millions of dollars in additional support. Similarly, trustees of a state university in the Rockies arranged to meet with key legislators, donors, faculty, and citizens-at-large both to convey the board's ambitions for the institution and to better understand constituents' expectations. Interactions like these, which place trustees at the crossroads of the organization and stakeholders, cultivate a sense of responsible trusteeship and, at the same time, provide board members with firsthand knowledge that enriches the board's deliberations in all three modes. In these and similar situations,

individual board members cannot, except at considerable personal embarrassment, simply plead ignorance about the organization's programs, finances, performance, and values.

A third approach relies on high-stakes issues, the hallmark of
Type III governance, rather than high-stakes situations. In this
scenario, the entire board works in breakout groups on the same
crucial assignment, for example, "How do we learn to look at
the organization through the eyes of key stakeholders?" or
"How do we reconcile the tension between deeply-rooted traditions and contemporary relevance?" (Type II questions might
be: "How do we reposition the organization in an ever more
competitive environment?" or "What metrics best capture organizational performance?") In smaller groups, trustees are more
likely to be prepared and productive; free riders have nowhere
to hide. Since every group has the identical assignment (unlike
regular committee work), when the board reconvenes all trustees
are better positioned to judge the quality of each group's work.
Substandard performance by one group will be instantly obser-
vable by the others. Colleagues will be disappointed, and the
laggards may be tacitly sanctioned and stigmatized. Equally important, the nonperformers will exert little influence as crucial
matters, like the institution's sense of self or the cornerstones of
the next strategic plan, are vigorously debated. Both substantively and procedurally, this arrangement fosters consequential
work and reinforces a common obligation to be diligent and to
deliver quality.

Executive sessions without the CEO present (something now
required of companies listed on the New York Stock Exchange)
offer a fourth mechanism to convert the trust generated by
social capital into constructively candid conversations. These
are occasions for the trustees, as peers, to be self-aware and self-

critical. "How have we performed as a group? Where have we lagged? How can we do better? Have we adhered to a norm of discourse and not a norm of consensus? Have we worked well in all three modes of governance?" Trustees are unlikely to address these questions as forthrightly in the presence of the CEO, at least until the board has become well-acclimated to a new norm of candor and self-reflection. But when trustworthiness permeates the social environment, trustees can more readily confront and correct subpar performance by the board.

Whatever the particular means to initiate and institutionalize self-regulated, self-enforced norms of diligence and rigor, social capital facilitates the process and offers boards a new and powerful resource to instill a keener sense of mutual obligation, a custom of critical inquiry, and a culture of accountability and productivity. These are desirable outcomes no matter what the mode of governance.

Without sufficient social capital, nonprofits are apt to focus on all manner of structural and technical devices—agendas, committees, bylaws, information systems, orientations, self-assessments—to improve board performance. Some incremental improvements will likely ensue. However, adjustments to board structure and operations will not resolve problems embedded in the board's values and culture. As Roger Raber, CEO and president of the National Association of Corporate Boards, observed at a seminar we convened, the most effective boards are "value-based, not rule based." Type III governance encourages and equips boards to frame and confront value-based questions and challenges throughout the organization. There is no place more appropriate for trustees to start than to attempt to make sense together of the board's purpose, persona, and performance, an admittedly tall task made markedly easier by a storehouse of social capital.

CAPITALIZING ON TRUSTEES

As responsible fiduciaries, trustees endeavor to conserve and enhance an organization's tangible assets like finances, facilities, endowment, and personnel. In the strategic mode, boards attempt to convert these same assets, as well as intangibles like organizational traditions, ethos, and image, into comparative advantage. Trustees have no less responsibility to extract maximum value from the board as from other organizational assets. And this value can be denominated in more currencies than financial capital.

In fact, if boards launched campaigns to cultivate and deploy the trustees' intellectual, reputational, political, and social capital that were roughly comparable to efforts to garner the trustees' financial resources, the results could yield substantial dividends. Both the organization and the board would be smarter, more respected, more influential, and better equipped to perceive and handle generative challenges. In short, the organization would be better governed.

CHAPTER 8

Where to Next?

In an ideal world, boards could approach governance as leadership with a blank slate. With a wave of the wand, all current board practices, structures, and traditions would disappear, along with all contrary habits of mind, troublesome group dynamics, and aversion to change. Since boards cannot start anew, they have to start where they are, and the first step in the process is to find out where that is. Toward that end, in this chapter we present three diagnostic exercises that can be used, in conjunction with the framework from Chapter 5, to help locate the board's current position; some observations about integrating governance as leadership into board structure, process, and leadership; and an assessment of the costs of practicing governance as leadership versus the costs of passing it up.

IS THE GAME WORTH THE CANDLE?

Readers who have come this far presumably believe that governance as leadership has value for boards and, ultimately, for nonprofit organizations. Of course, we agree, and at the end of Chapter 6 we summarized the benefits of generative governance. However, this new approach entails some risk, as skeptics will be quick to note. We will enumerate the potential costs of governance as leadership after we consider a less obvious corollary: the costs attached to the status quo.

For the many boards beset by problems of purpose, the costs of business as usual are enormous. The irrelevance, detachment, and underutilization of trustees lead to accountability failures; the boards most disengaged by inconsequential work are least able to sustain the vigilance needed for effective oversight. And problems of purpose can also impose costly dysfunctions on the organization. In search of meaningful work, frustrated trustees sometimes meddle in management. This exasperates executives and intensifies resentment among the staff, which often feels obliged, if only for purposes of political survival, to create the illusion that the board is both valuable and valued.

The opportunity costs of the status quo are also considerable. As boards pursue insignificant work, organizations squander trustee value. As consultants, we frequently ask trustees to rate their board's performance on a scale of "A" to "F." Most boards average a "B," though we suspect from trustees' self-criticisms that this grade may be an inflated equivalent of a "gentleman's C": just good enough to pass. When we ask trustees to describe the differences between an "A" board and a "B" or "C" board, most intuitively grasp the differences and recognize the gulf between the board's performance and potential, even when they are unclear about how to close the gap. Although these discussions indicate that many trustees perceive that the board's potential often goes untapped, more than a few nonprofit boards and staff are nonetheless hesitant to "tamper" with governance.

In fact, many feel compelled to follow the beaten path, blinded to choice by one of the great paradoxes of organizational life: the less certain they are about how to handle a challenge, the more likely they are to imitate others. The result is perverse: Everyone in a particular field (for example, nonprofit governance) chooses the same form, not because they know what works, but because they do not.[1] Organizations, in effect, find safety in numbers; no one can be too critical of a board that follows well-established conventions and generally accepted practices. Generative thinking leads in the opposite direction. The more ambiguity and uncertainty, the greater the need for boards to frame and make choices in light of the organization's sense of self and sense of circumstances. When that leads trustees to depart from the most conventional practice of trusteeship, the board may well be subject to more scrutiny both inside and outside the organization.

In addition to this risk, trustees partial to governance as leadership will have to learn new ways that disrupt old habits, and change rarely happens without stress, disagreement, and resistance. Beyond the scrutiny and anxiety that accompany change, trustees and executives can anticipate three start-up challenges. None is inevitable, but all require vigilance which, in turn, exacts a price.

First, some boards and CEOs may be inclined to pursue the advice we offer too literally. This would be a mistake. We do not recommend, for instance, that boards predetermine or budget the amount of time to be spent in each mode of governance, either overall or on a specific issue. This would be as wrongheaded as a CEO deciding in advance to be a mentor 10 percent of the time, a visionary 20 percent, a mediator 30 percent, and a manager the rest of the time. Boards must work in each

---

[1]This phenomenon has been termed "isomorphism." See DiMaggio and Powell, 1991.

mode as circumstances warrant, and learn through reflection, deliberation, and experience to move seamlessly from one mode to another, just as an effective chief executive in the span of an hour or two moves from power broker to motivator, mentor, manager, and leader.

Second, organizations need to guard against unproductive overuse of a mode, particularly the generative mode. Boards and staff would be paralyzed if each and every item on an agenda were deconstructed to locate some elusive generative core. To reiterate, some technical problems are just that and should be dispatched as expeditiously as possible. A board need not return to square one, or the top of the generative curve, to address a purely fiduciary matter or deal with the development, modification, or implementation of a strategic plan that was the outgrowth of prior generative work. We have no ready rule of thumb here; only self-awareness on the part of trustees and staff will ensure that the board does not overcomplicate simple issues or oversimplify complicated ones.

Third, governance as leadership could easily become the pretext for "reforms" (more accurately, hobbyhorses) that various trustees or staff have long been eager to advance. Cohen and March (1974) colorfully described this phenomenon as a "garbage can" choice model—where people metaphorically dump all sorts of accumulated problems and solutions, usually unrelated to one another, into new and attractive decision-making bins. Changes in board governance thus become the excuse to entertain changes in organizational programs, executive compensation plans, investment managers, mission statements, or any other "problem" a trustee wants to attach to a new "solution." Governance as leadership has real value, though not as the solution to every problem encountered by every member of every board.

On balance, the possible pitfalls of governance as leadership are more than offset by the potential benefits, especially when we add the costs associated with the status quo. So if the rewards are worth the risks, what is next?

DIAGNOSTICS

If governance as leadership were about new configurations of board tasks and structures, the game plan would be easy to write. Indeed, some prescriptive literature has the flavor of five (or six or four) easy steps to better governance: a nip of structure here and a tuck of process there and, *voilà*, we have a new and improved board. Governance as leadership, by contrast, constitutes a new *understanding* of purposes and modes; trustees and executives cannot simply implement enlightenment. Their challenge is to understand how, as a board and a CEO, they now make sense of governance and what kind of trusteeship that sense has created. This understanding, in turn, can help a board assess how and where it needs to focus in pursuing governance as leadership.

Diagnostic exercises are more apt than tool kits to advance this process. We offer three. The first exercise explores the board's purpose in governing, the second the board's value in governing, and the third the trustees' satisfaction from governing. All three entail self-study, but not in the manner of standard board self-assessments that ask trustees to rate, on a scale from 1–5 (Poor to Excellent), the board's performance. These conventional approaches help trustees measure their performance against traditional notions of trusteeship, both conceptually (Does the board clearly delegate authority to management?) and operationally (Does the board review the organization's mission statement annually?). The results are tabulated, the scores are averaged, and the board's "grades" are revealed. Under the best conditions, the board then tries to do better what some prototype of trusteeship suggests that boards should do well.

This approach may serve reasonably well Type I and Type II *boards* that hew closely to traditional notions of trusteeship. But consistent with the principles of the generative mode, governance as leadership requires more opportunity for the board to make sense of trusteeship, not to make grades. These diagnostic exercises, therefore, are a little bit more like Rorshach tests and a little less like machine-scored tests.

Exercise 1: The purpose of governing. If trustees were to literally ask each other, "What constitutes governance?," the answers would likely be a recitation of the board's official job description. To uncover the personal visions of trusteeship that profoundly shape the way boards work, trustees need to dig deeper. We have asked groups of trustees (as well as executives and consultants to boards) to create analogies that capture the essential relationship between a nonprofit board and a nonprofit organization. Specifically, trustees are asked to complete this statement: "Board is to organization as _____ is to _____." The results reveal how people make sense of a board's purpose and place in an organization. In fact, we discovered that, without mention of the tri-modal model, others implicitly recognized that boards operate in multiple modes. The answers can be categorized fairly neatly across the three modes. Exhibit 8.1 arrays some representative responses.

A board can readily replicate this exercise by asking each trustee to create one analogy that best describes the board's cur-

EXHIBIT 8.1	ANALOGIES

Board is to organization as...

Type I: Board as Control Mechanism	Type II: Board as Direction-Setter	Type III: Board as Meaning-Maker
dam : river	compass : navigation	inspiration : poet
curbstone : roadway	headlights : automobile	values : choices
border collie : cattle herd	rudder : boat	designer : work of art
air traffic controller : pilots	guidance system : satellite	conscience : ethical person
governor : engine	periscope : submarine	spirit : higher purpose
inspector : passport	flight planner : pilot	vision : implementation
operating system : computer		norms : group dynamics
landlord : tenant		

rent relationship to the organization, and another that reflects a more desirable connection. The responses can be classified across the three modes, and then used to spark discussion about how the board understands the purpose of governance. For example, do we envision purposes in all three modes? Some more than others? Do we have a shared sense about the purposes of governance? How large a gap exists between the board's current sense of governance and governance as leadership?

Trustees should also be on the lookout for a danger signal: analogies which suggest a passive role for the board. For example, board is to organization as:

canary : coal mine

canvas : creative expression

computer : software
king : parliament
safety net : trapeze artist
trees : paper mill

Exercise 2: The value in governing. Trustees need to distinguish between the work a board does and work essential to governing. The board's work spans a continuum from helpful work (for example, *pro bono* consulting) that is not critical to governing; to technical work critical to governing; to highly generative work equally, or even more, essential to governing.

To discover how much of which type of work the board does, ask each trustee to sort the board's work (or, as appropriate, the committee's work) into one of three categories:

1. *Work that requires* no *board.* What elements of the board's work could be delegated to others—staff, consultants, or board members acting in an unofficial capacity—with little or no effect on the governance of the organization?

2. *Work that requires* a *board.* What elements of the board's work can be handled *only* by an official board? To think of this another way, imagine a "board swap" where two equally competent boards of different organizations trade places. What types of work would both boards, in their new organization, be able to perform proficiently? Where are boards basically interchangeable?

3. *Work that requires* this *board:* With the "board swap" still in mind, what work would the new board now governing your organization perform least capably?

Exhibit 8.2 provides some sample responses.

The goal of this exercise is *not* for boards to shed less essential work, although that may be a by-product. Nor do we sug-

EXHIBIT 8.2	VALUABLE WORK

Work that requires *no* board	Work that requires *a* board	Work that requires *this* board
Providing management help, *pro bono* consulting. Developing rules like library fines, parking regulations, visiting hours	Receiving and reviewing the annual audit. Ensuring a balanced budget. Approving a contract with a vendor.	Hiring the right CEO. Interacting with key constituents. Deciding if a proposal is consistent with our mission and values.

gest that boards "outsource" critically important fiduciary functions (for example, the review of budgets and audits) to the lowest qualified bidder. Rather, the exercise encourages boards to identify the most essential governing work—work that requires *this* board—and to then devote as much time and attention as possible to these truly essential, high value-added activities.

Exercise 3: The satisfaction in governing. Governance as leadership rests on the assumption that governing can and should be consequential *and* engaging. Important but tedious work alone leads to the substitute's dilemma. Inconsequential but appealing work leads to illusory governance. Trustees need to determine what work the board does, or might do, that contributes significantly to both fulfillment of the organization's mission *and* trustee satisfaction.

To answer this question, trustees should ponder the following questions and then record their answers briefly on index cards:

- *Actual work.* On what work has the board spent the most time in the past year?

- *Valuable work.* What aspects of the board's work are most important to the organization's success or mission? Stated another way, what would be the gravest consequences to this organization if the board did not meet or function in any way for two years? (Assume this presented no legal problems and that there would be an administrative mechanism to approve an annual operating budget.)
- *Meaningful work.* What work would you most miss if the board decided not to do it or to have someone else do it?

Collect and randomly redistribute the cards (Exhibit 8.3 presents some illustrative answers). For each question, have all the responses read aloud, with similar answers clustered under an appropriate rubric or theme (for example, strategic planning, meeting with constituents).

EXHIBIT 8.3   VALUABLE AND MEANINGFUL WORK

Actual work	Valuable work	Meaningful work
Attending board and committee meetings	Working on and completing the capital campaign	Interacting with constituents
Authorizing a capital campaign	Hiring a new CEO	Identifying and working to solve really important issues—like how we're going to increase participation in our programs
Hiring a new CEO		Our annual retreat, where we discuss the issues we should be working on to advance the organization
		Hiring a new CEO

To stimulate discussion, trustees can ask: *What tensions and contradictions do our answers suggest?* In an ideal scenario, boards would hit a "trifecta," where their work is:

1. Indispensable to governing
2. Valuable to the organization
3. Satisfying to trustees

More realistically, there will not be a perfect correspondence. For example, boards might note activities that create value for the organization but do not especially gratify trustees. In the worst case, the lion's share of what the board does would be of little value to either the organization or the trustees. Here lie opportunities for addition by subtraction.

When taken together, these three diagnostic exercises will provide an instructive picture of the board's current state of governance. Based on the overall pattern of responses, trustees can ask: What do we need to do to move closer to governance as leadership? Are we mired in one mode? Do we fit squarely within one quadrant in the generative governing framework presented in Chapter 5 (Exhibit 5.2): Or do we straddle the boundaries between two quadrants?

Another way to learn to what extent the board currently engages in generative work would be for the trustees and executives to address some or all of these questions:

- Can we cite examples of occasions when we worked in each of the three modes? Did we take a "triple- (or even double-) helix" approach to any issue? (See p. 109.)
- Is there evidence that we are a Type I, II, or III *board* rather than a board that moves deftly between Type I, II, and III *work?*

- What important assets of the issues we addressed might have been illuminated if we had governed in a different or additional mode?
- How were the issues before us framed, and by whom?
- Did we overlook better, deeper questions because we bypassed the generative mode?

Now the board has a well-developed sense of whether it practices governance as leadership and, if so, how effectively. Where results fall short of the trustees' standards or expectations, the board can revisit the suggestions offered in the previous chapters to improve performance in each of the three modes.

"ATTRACTIVE NUISANCES"

Governance as leadership will be facilitated by the many practical measures we presented earlier in this chapter and in Chapters 3, 4, and 6. For example, we recommended that the structure and agendas of committees be tied to strategy, that meetings be conducted so as to encourage generative thinking, and that trustees work at organizational boundaries. However, we know from experience that there are a few other issues that consume trustee attention but that are not, in reality, central to successful governance as leadership, or at least not in the way most trustees think. We call these "attractive nuisances," which, in legal parlance, denotes a "dangerous condition that might attract children onto land thereby subjecting them to the risk of that danger."[2] In this instance, the parties at risk are trustees, not children, and the attractive nuisances are not unfenced swim-

---

[2]www.legal-definitions.com

ming pools or unrestrained pets but three perennially debated questions of board design: board size, board composition, and trustee term limits.

Board size. Over the years, we have come to a simple realization: Most small boards would like to be larger and most large boards would like to be smaller. In other words, one board's problem is another board's solution.

Trustees and managers are convinced that board size significantly influences board performance, but we have seen boards of all sizes that are effective and ineffective, engaged and disengaged, incredibly valuable or nearly worthless. For example, many small boards want to be larger in order to raise money, confer greater legitimacy, add diversity, or expand constituent involvement. Many large boards would prefer to be smaller in order to encourage engagement, prevent "free riders," and enhance collegiality.

Discussions of size may be a convenient way to sidestep discussions of purpose and excuse mediocre performance. A board can be small and the organization can still raise money (for example, Harvard, Yale, the Getty Museum). A smaller, stellar board might signal greater legitimacy and execute more effectively than a huge board of superstars that exists mostly on letterhead. Similarly, there are many large boards that manage to keep trustees very much engaged through devices such as consequential work in small groups, structured opportunities to maximize participation, active feedback loops, rotational leadership, and constant socialization (and resocialization) of members to group norms. Irrespective of size, a board needs to:

- Have sufficient hands and minds to do the essential, non-substitutable work of governance in all three modes.

- Avoid the substitute's dilemma, where asking little of trustees begets even less.
- Provide multiple opportunities to offer multiple perspectives that elicit alternative ways to frame issues and prevent "groupthink."

Bigger and smaller boards will approach these functions differently. However, just as functional families, large and small, learn to adjust successfully to size, so too can boards of trustees. A larger board needs particularly skillful leadership that fosters participation. Board, committee, and task force chairs must make sure that quiet voices are not overwhelmed by loud ones, and that the one person who has doubts about a proposed course of action can express those reservations without hesitancy (and perhaps prevent a big mistake). A large board also has greater need for breakout groups to increase available airtime, to allow unformed ideas to emerge, and to instill a sense of accountability. At the same time, a small board should be alert to the dangers of "groupthink" and perhaps more open to multi-constituent task forces, focus groups, and other mechanisms to solicit a wide and representative range of views.

Trustees tempted to dwell on the size of the board should ask "What would we do differently or better tomorrow if the size of the board were, instantly, what we regard as optimal? What would we do worse?" Start with results and work backward. "What impedes the outcomes we seek? Why can other boards, comparable in size to this board, achieve these results?" Size does not matter nearly as much as some imagine. The size of a board affects how a board works more than how well it works.

Board Composition. Nonprofits too often consider ideal board composition to be the equivalent of a versatile small appliance, sold on late-night television, that slices and dices, chops, shreds, minces, and juliennes—and it's dishwasher-safe, too! The board-as-multipurpose-appliance includes a mix of technical expertise, wealth, diversity, and political connections. But trustees expressly recruited for technical expertise (for example, law, banking, engineering) are likely, either as a matter of preference or at management's direction, to concentrate on technical aspects of the organization. Trustees recruited principally as constituent representatives or as tokens of diversity are frequently marginalized as stakeholder advocates or symbolic placeholders. And well-heeled board members recruited as attractive development prospects may expect to exert disproportionate influence over matters large and small in exchange for largess. In short, this type of board-as-Swiss-army-knife has been recruited to do everything *but* govern.[3]

The more that boards gravitate toward governance as leadership, the more this vacuum will be apparent and problematic. Technical expertise, wealth, and connections are all still necessary, though no longer sufficient. How trustees think becomes more important than what trustees know. Technical expertise can always be acquired on the outside; the vital work that needs to be done at the top of the generative curve cannot be so easily outsourced. In Type III mode, other forms of capital (for example, intellectual, reputational, political, and social), as described in Chapter 7, assume an importance at least commensurate with financial capital. And the ability to represent the

---

[3]These considerations would be different, of course, if we were addressing the challenges of all-volunteer or very young nonprofits with little staff capacity. But as we noted in the preface, our analysis is aimed at nonprofits with professional staff and volunteer boards.

board at the boundaries of the organization becomes more critical than a determination to represent a constituency to the board.

In sum, governance as leadership suggests a new approach to trustee recruitment, one that stresses quality of mind, a tolerance for ambiguity, an appetite for organizational puzzles, a fondness for robust discourse, and a commitment to team play.

While the old checklists, centered around trustees' personal, professional, and financial background, may still have some utility, these new criteria deserve equal or greater weight. Otherwise, the organization may find itself with a board that plays many, indeed *any*, useful roles, other than the most important one: to contribute leadership through the practice of governance.

Trustee Term limits. Term limits pose the same dilemma as board size. There are trade-offs that periodically tempt boards to swap one set of problems for another. Term limits solve the problem of "deadwood" but create the problem of costly turnover among valued and dedicated trustees. Without term limits, boards avert that risk but suffer instead from an inability to remove the laggards and infuse the board with "new blood." These are all legitimate worries that cannot be solved just by changing the bylaws, whether to institute or abolish term limits.

Well done, governance as leadership can moderate, though not cure, the drawbacks that each of these alternatives presents. Boards without term limits need to keep trustees engaged and fresh year after year. With a focus on learning, framing, generating, interacting, and resolving, governance as leadership will keep trustees engrossed longer, more passionately, and more profitably for the organization. Generative work promotes the discovery of new problems and opportunities and stimulates a plurality of perspectives. Anchored to consequential work by the board and often with other stakeholders, governance as leadership ups the ante and heightens accountability in ways that alleviate the "free rider" problem.

At the same time, a board with term limits, but engaged in generative governance, has two powerful magnets to draw new trustees: (1) a meaningful role in consequential work and (2) the testimony of fulfilled ex–board members. If the challenges and opportunities inherent to Type III governance prove irresistible to a recruit, then the chances for a productive tenure are excellent. Conversely, potential trustees, daunted by the prospect of governance that demands much so that board members contribute even more, can opt out, to the advantage of the organization and the would-be trustee.

A NEW COVENANT

Governance as leadership carries an implied bargain: more macrogovernance in exchange for less micromanagement. For this arrangement to work, neither the board nor management can accept the "*quid*" but withhold the "*quo*." In other words, the board cannot move toward to the top of the generative curve, where issues are framed, and at the same time remain as active at the bottom of the curve where strategic plans and technical tasks are executed. Likewise, executives cannot "evict" the board from the zone of micromanagement without some other place for the trustees to go, namely the realm of generative governance.

This new covenant asks a great deal of both parties. At first, trustees may be energized by the possibility that the dreary work of conventional governance will be replaced by countless opportunities to explore, intuit, improvise, dissent, and even engage in "playful" discussions. But the real picture is more complex. With this new freedom to be generative comes an obligation to be equal to the challenge.

Governance as leadership is not a license for boards to govern anywhere, any time, any way. To the contrary, this new approach requires more self-discipline and collective responsibility of board members than traditional governance does. If, as most trustees fervently believe, leadership matters immensely then, by definition, governance as leadership matters immensely, too. Therefore, board members need to come prepared, rise to the occasion, work diligently as a group, and expect to be intellectually taxed by complex and consequential questions. Most trustees will recognize these specifications as the price one pays to do meaningful work, and as the very same expectations that board members have of colleagues in their own work environment.

The challenges that governance as leadership pose for executives are more about sharing, not assuming, greater responsibility. Whether in response to the board's signals, personal preference, or socialization by peers, executives are often cast as lonely heroes who have nearly all the answers nearly all the time. In the minds of many CEOs and board members, for a leader to admit to confusion or uncertainty—or, worse, to have no idea what to do—conveys weakness or incompetence. As a result, executives frequently do alone generative work that is better done with the board.

With governance as leadership, the capacity to *share* this work with the board ranks among the executive's major contributions. The CEO exposes, and even more to the point, immerses the board in complex and critical matters as issues arise and unfold. In addition, the CEO describes, rather than suppresses, dimly perceived concerns that incite an instinctive wariness. In the generative discussions that follow, the CEO (and senior staff) are secure enough to be open to argument and susceptible to influence without concern for who "wins" or "loses" the debate or who "wins" or "loses" power. The quality and value of the conversation are the litmus tests that count.

The CEO still stands as *the* leader of the organization and still provides leadership for the board. However, that leadership now engages and challenges the board, whereas CEOs may once have been inclined to marginalize or shield the board. Will there be, now and then, untidiness and moments when the CEO feels some loss of control? Certainly. But just as other professionals— whether athletes, professors, lawyers, or actors—perform better when surrounded by talented peers, executives who seriously engage boards and boards that demand serious engagement will govern more effectively. The less an organization depends on a lonely and heroic leader, the more leadership and the better governance the organization will have.

COMING FULL CIRCLE

A little bit of governance as leadership is worse than none at all. Yet, for different reasons, trustees and executives may both prefer governance-as-leadership "lite." Some trustees may relish occasions to share their generative genius with the CEO and staff for a few hours every time the board meets. But generative work, without strategic or fiduciary work, can lapse all too quickly into self-absorbed navel-gazing. Work in all three modes, as we have stressed from the outset, keeps generative work grounded in organizational realities.

Executives, too, might be tempted to go halfway with governance as leadership. Some will incline to engage in generative work but keep the board at bay. There might be a little generative discussion from time to time about how management frames issues, but there would be no robust exchanges and no searches for other frames. Management might provide some glimpses into the organization's culture, core competencies, and competitive advantage, but there would be few opportunities for the board, as a whole, to do an "independent study" at the boundaries of the organization. Skillful and persistent CEOs can dilute (or even thwart) governance as leadership, but as we cautioned in the previous chapter, to do so courts a significant risk. Halfway measures may authorize trustees to frame the organization's challenges and opportunities, but without adequate knowledge of the organization's values, beliefs, assumptions, and traditions. As a result, executives may get plenty of frames but very little framing. Far better, we believe, for executives to have partial control of a complete perspective than complete control of a partial perspective.

We believe that nonprofit boards face a problem of purpose, not a problem of performance. When organizations reframe governance as leadership, the board becomes more than a fiduciary of tangible assets and more than management's strategic partner, as vital as those functions are. The board also becomes a crucial and generative source of leadership for the organization. In short, the board learns to perform effectively in all three modes of governance. The better trustees do that, the more deeply the board will understand the purpose of governance. And the better the board understands governance, the better governed the organization will be. This is not a vicious circle; it is the cycle of successful governance.

References

Andrews, K. R. (1971). *The Concept of Corporate Strategy.* Homewood, IL: Richard D. Irwin, Inc.

Baldridge, J. V., Curtis, D. V., Ecker, G., and Riley, G. L. (1978). *Policy Making and Effective Leadership.* San Francisco: Jossey-Bass.

Birnbaum, R. (1988a). *How Colleges Work: The Cybernetics of Academic Organization and Leadership* (1st ed.). San Francisco: Jossey-Bass.

Birnbaum, R. (1988b). Presidential Searches and the Discovery of Organizational Goals. *Journal of Higher Education, 59*(5), 489–509.

Birnbaum, R. (1992). *How Academic Leadership Works: Understanding Success and Failure in the College Presidency* (1st ed.). San Francisco: Jossey-Bass.

Birnbaum, R. (2000). *Management Fads in Higher Education.* San Francisco: Jossey-Bass.

Bolman, L. G., and Deal, T. E. (1997). *Reframing Organizations: Artistry, Choice, and Leadership* (2nd ed.). San Francisco: Jossey-Bass Publishers.

Brown, P. L. (2002, May 8). Megachurches as Minitowns. *New York Times,* pp. D1, D4.

Chait, R. P., Holland, T. P., and Taylor, B. E. (1993). *The Effective Board of Trustees.* Phoenix, AZ: American Council on Education and The Oryx Press.

Chait, R. P., Holland, T. P., and Taylor, B. E. (1996). *Improving the Performance of Governing Boards.* Phoenix, AZ: American Council on Education and The Oryx Press.

Chait, R. P., and Taylor, B. E. (1989). Charting the Territory of Nonprofit Boards. *Harvard Business Review* (January–February).

Christensen, C. M. (1997). *The Innovator's Dilemma: When New Technologies Cause Great Firms to Fail.* Boston: Harvard Business School Press.

Clark, B. R. (1972). The Organizational Saga in Higher Education. *Administrative Science Quarterly,* 17(2).

Cohen, M. D., and March, J. G. (1974). *Leadership and Ambiguity: The American College President.* New York: McGraw-Hill Book Company.

Collins, J. (2001). *Good to Great: Why Some Companies Make the Leap ... and Others Don't.* New York: HarperBusiness.

Collins, J., and Porras, J. (1994). *Built to Last: Successful Habits of Visionary Companies.* New York: HarperBusiness.

Csikszentmihalyi, M. (2003). *Good Business: Leadership, Flow, and the Making of Meaning.* New York: Viking Penguin.

Deal, T. E., and Kennedy, A. A. (1982). *Corporate Cultures: The Rites and Rituals of Corporate Life.* Reading, MA: Addison-Wesley Publishing Company, Inc.

Deschamps, J. P., and Nayak, P. R. (1995). *Product Juggernauts: How Companies Mobilize to Generate a Stream of Market Winners.* Boston: Harvard Business School Press.

Dewan, S. K. (2004, April 28). New York's Gospel of Policing by Data Spreads Across U.S. *New York Times,* p. A1.

DiMaggio, P. J., and Powell, W. W. (1991). The Iron Cage Revisited: Institutional Isomorphism and Collective Rationality in Organizational Fields. In P. J. DiMaggio and W. W. Powell (Eds.), *The New Institutionalism in Organizational Analysis* (pp. 63–82). Chicago: University of Chicago Press.

Dubner, S. (2003, June 28). Calculating the Irrational in Economics. *New York Times,* p. B7.

Edgers, G. (2004, February 15). Art Fans Take a Vegas Vacation. *Boston Globe,* pp. N1, N4.

Fleishman, J. (1999). Public Trust in Not-for-Profit Organizations and the Need for Regulatory Reform. In C. T. Clotfelter and

T. Ehrlich (Eds.), *Philanthropy and the Nonprofit Sector in a Changing America* (pp. 172–197). Bloomington, IN: Indiana University Press.

Fremont-Smith, M. R. (2004). *Governing Nonprofit Organizations: Federal and State Law and Regulation*. Cambridge, MA: Belknap Press of Harvard University Press.

Fuerbringer, J. (1997, March 30). Why Both Bulls and Bears Can Act So Bird-Brained. *New York Times*, p. 1.

Gardner, H. (1983). *Frames of Mind: The Theory of Multiple Intelligences*. New York: Basic Books.

Gardner, H. (1993). *Creating Minds: An Anatomy of Creativity Seen Through the Lives of Freud, Einstein, Picasso, Stravinsky, Eliot, Graham, and Gandhi*. New York: Basic Books.

Gardner, H., in collaboration with Emma Laskin. (1995). *Leading Minds: An Anatomy of Leadership*. New York: Basic Books.

Gergen, D., and Kellerman, B. (2000). Pain Management. *Compass: A Journal of Leadership*, 1(2), 40.

Golden, D. (2002, April 29). In Effort to Lift Their Rankings, Colleges Recruit Jewish Students. *Wall Street Journal*, pp. A1, A8.

Goleman, D. (1995). *Emotional Intelligence: Why It Can Matter More than IQ*. New York: Bantam.

Gonzalez, D. (2003, June 14). Holding On to Beliefs Despite the Insistence of Fact. *New York Times*, p. B1.

Hamel, G. (1996). Strategy as Revolution. *Harvard Business Review* (July–August).

Hamel, G., and Prahalad, C. K. (1997). *Competing for the Future*. Boston: Harvard Business School Press.

Heifetz, R. A. (1994). *Leadership without Easy Answers*. Cambridge, MA: Belknap Press of Harvard University Press.

Herzlinger, R. (1997). *Market Driven Health Care*. Cambridge, MA: Perseus Books.

Heskett, J. (1987). Lessons in the Service Sector. *Harvard Business Review* (March–April).

Houle, C. O. (1960). *The Effective Board*. New York: Association Press.

Houle, C. O. (1989). *Governing Boards: Their Nature and Nurture*. San Francisco: Jossey-Bass.

Hughes, S. R., Lakey, B. M., and Bobowick, M. J. (2000). *The Board Building Cycle: Nine Steps to Finding, Recruiting, and Engaging Nonprofit Board Members*. Washington, D.C.: BoardSource.

Jackson, K. T. (2004). *Building Reputational Capital—Strategies for Integrity and Fair Play That Improve the Bottom Line*. Oxford: Oxford University Press.

Janis, I. L. (1982). *Groupthink: Psychological Studies of Policy Decisions and Fiascoes*. Boston: Houghton Mifflin.

Julius, D., Baldridge, J. V., and Pfeffer, J. (1999). A Memo for Machiavelli. *Journal of Higher Education* (March–April), 113–133.

Kanter, R. M. (1983). *The Change Masters: Innovation & Entrepreneurship in the American Corporation*. New York: Simon & Schuster, Inc.

Kaplan, R. S., and Norton, D. P. (1996). *The Balanced Scorecard: Translating Strategy into Action*. Boston: Harvard Business School Press.

Kelling, G. L., and Coles, C. M. (1996). *Fixing Broken Windows: Restoring Order and Reducing Crime in Our Communities*. New York: Touchstone Press.

Kolata, G. (1996, April 12). The Long Shelf Life of Medical Myths. *New York Times*, p. 2.

Kotler, P., and Murphy, P. (1991). Strategic Planning for Higher Education. In M. Peterson (Ed.), *ASHE Reader on Organization and Governance in Higher Education* (4th ed.). Needham Heights, MA: Ginn.

Learning from Nonprofits. (1990, March 26). *Business Week*, 66–74.

Letts, C. W., Ryan, W. P., and Grossman, A. (1999). *High-Performance Nonprofit Organizations: Managing Upstream for Great Impact*. New York: John Wiley & Sons.

Lewontin, R. (2000). *The Triple Helix: Gene, Organism, and Environment*. Cambridge, MA: Harvard University Press.

Lorsch, J. W., and Maciver, E. (2000). *Pawns or Potentates: The Reality of America's Corporate Boards*. Cambridge, MA: Harvard Business School Press.

Mace, M. (1971). *Directors: Myth and Reality*. Cambridge, MA: Harvard Business School Press.

Massey, D. (2002, July 12). What People Just Don't Understand About Academic Fields. *The Chronicle of Higher Education*, p. B4.

Mellado, J. (1991). "Willow Creek Community Church." Boston: Harvard Business School Publishing.

Mintzberg, H. (1994). *The Rise and Fall of Strategic Planning: Reconceiving Roles for Planning, Plans, Planners*. New York: Free Press.

Mintzberg, H. (1998). *Strategy Safari: A Guided Tour Through the Wilds of Strategic Planning*. New York: Free Press.

Morgan, G. (1997). *Images of Organization* (2nd ed.). Thousand Oaks, CA: Sage Publications.

Pfeffer, J. (1981). *Power in Organizations*. Boston: Pitman.

Pfeffer, J. (1992). *Managing with Power: Politics and Influence in Organizations*. Boston: Harvard Business School Press.

Polanyi, M. (1974). *Personal Knowledge*. Chicago: University of Chicago Press.

Porter, M. E. (1980). *Competitive Strategy: Techniques for Analyzing Industries and Competitors*. New York: The Free Press.

Porter, M. E. (1996). What Is Strategy? *Harvard Business Review* (November–December), 61–78.

Robert III, S. C., Evans, W. J., Honemann, D. H., and Balch, T. J. (2000). *Robert's Rules of Order Newly Revised* (10th ed.). New York: Perseus Books.

Schein, E. H. (1992). *Organizational Culture and Leadership* (2nd ed.). San Francisco: Jossey-Bass Publishers.

Schein, E. H. (1993). How Can Organizations Learn Faster? The Challenge of Entering the Green Room. *Sloan Management Review* (Winter), 85–92.

Schmidtlein, F. (1988). College and University Planning: Perspectives from a Nationwide Study. *Planning for Higher Education*, 17(3).

Schon, D. A. (1983). *The Reflective Practitioner: How Professionals Think in Action*. London: Temple Smith.

Scott, W. R. (2003). *Organizations: Rational, Natural, and Open Systems* (5th ed.). Upper Saddle River, NJ: Prentice-Hall.

Senge, P. (1990). *The Fifth Discipline: The Art and Practice of the Learning Organization.* New York: Doubleday/Currency.

Shapiro, E. C. (1995). *Fad Surfing in the Boardroom.* Reading, MA: Addison-Wesley Publishing Company, Inc.

Smith, D. H. (1995). *Entrusted: The Moral Responsibilities of Trusteeship.* Bloomington, IN: Indiana University Press.

Spontaneous Generation. (2004). *Encyclopædia Britannica Premium Service,* 2004.

Stacey, R. D. (1996). *Complexity and Creativity in Organizations.* San Francisco: Berrett-Koehler Publishers.

Stewart, T. A. (1997). *Intellectual Capital: The New Wealth of Organizations.* New York: Doubleday.

Taylor, B. E., Chait, R. P., and Holland, T. P. (1991). Trustee Motivation and Board Effectiveness. *Nonprofit and Voluntary Sector Quarterly,* 20(2), 207–224.

Taylor, B. E., Chait, R. P., and Holland, T. P. (1996). The New Work of the Nonprofit Board. *Harvard Business Review* (September–October).

Taylor, B. E., and Massy, W. F. (1996). *Strategic Indicators for Higher Education.* Princeton, NJ: Peterson's.

Volunteer Protection Act of 1997, Public Law 105–119 (1997).

Watson, G. H. (1993). *Strategic Benchmarking: How to Rate Your Company's Performance Against the World's Best.* New York: John Wiley & Sons.

Weick, K. E. (1976). Educational Organizations as Loosely Coupled Systems. *Administrative Science Quarterly,* 21, 1–19.

Weick, K. E. (1995). *Sensemaking in Organizations.* Thousand Oaks, CA: Sage Publications.

Zimmerman, B., Lindberg, C., and Plsek, P. (1998). *Edgeware: Insights from Complexity Science for Health Care Leaders.* Irving, TX: VHA Inc.

Index